PATHS OF LEADERSHIP

Guiding Others toward Growth in Christ through
SERVING
FOLLOWING
TEACHING
MODELING
ENVISIONING

Andrew T. Le Peau

InterVarsity Press
Downers Grove
Illinois 60515

InterVarsity Press is the book-publishing division of Inter-Varsity Christian Fellowship, a student movement active on campus at hundreds of universities, colleges and schools of nursing. For information about local and regional activities, write IVCF, 233 Langdon St., Madison, WI 53703.

Distributed in Canada through InterVarsity Press, 860 Denison St., Unit 3, Markham, Ontario L3R 4H1, Canada.

All quotation from the Scripture, unless otherwise noted, are from the Revised Standard Version of the Bible, copyright 1946, 1952, © *1971, 1973.*

Cover photograph: Robert McKendrick

ISBN 0-87784-806-8

Printed in the United States of America

Library of Congress Cataloging in Publication Data
Le Peau, Andrew T., 1952-
    Paths of leadership.

    Includes bibliographical references.
        1. Christian leadership.   2. Christian life—
1960-   I. Title.
BV652.1.L38   1983   248.4   82-23221
ISBN 0-87784-806-8

18	17	16	15	14	13	12	11	10	9	8	7	6	5	4	3	2	1
96	95	94	93	92	91	90	89	88	87	86	85	84	83				

To Phyllis, my love

1
Paths
of
Leadership

May the road rise to meet you.
Traditional Irish Blessing

There are as many definitions of leadership as there are people to lead. Harry Truman, in his typical straightforward style, once said, "A leader is a person who has the ability to get others to do what they don't want to do, and like it." But we often have the uncomfortable feeling that leaders get us to do these things for their good and not ours. We suspect we're being manipulated, but we follow anyway—because we like it.

A contemporary of Truman, Mahatma Gandhi identified tenacity as the key element: "To put up with these misrepresentations and to stick to one's guns come what might—this is the essence of leadership." Hannibal, as he contemplated crossing the Alps, typified this attitude: "I will find a way or make one."

The Roman historian Tacitus, however, held that "reason and calm judgment are the qualities of a leader," while Napoleon, the great French emperor, believed "a leader is a dealer in hope." Yet again, the ancient Chinese philosopher Lao-tse said, "A leader is best when people barely know he exists."

The Bible too has much to say about leadership. Paul affirmed its value when he told Timothy, "To aspire to leadership is an honourable ambition" (1 Tim 3:1 NEB). In fact he gave Timothy and Titus the very job of appointing elders.

The Bible is full of leaders. We see planners like Joseph and Nehemiah who guided men and women in huge public works projects extending over many years. We see military strategists like Joshua and David who helped form ancient Israel into a nation. We see courageous women like Deborah and Esther who saved their people with acts of high heroism. We see prophets like Jeremiah and Amos whose public ministry seemed to have little impact but whose inner lives became fortresses for God. We see parents like Hannah and Moses' mother who both gave up their children to God under very different circumstances but whose influence was exerted, nonetheless, on their sons who both became mighty men of Israel. Administrators, soldiers, prophets, parents—all leaders. All men and women of God. Yet all very different in their personalities and powers.

But we come back to square one. With all these differences, what is a leader? And more specifically, for that is the topic of this book, what is a spiritual leader? How do we help others grow in Christ? My working definition is this: Leadership is any influence any person has on an individual or group to meet its needs or goals for the glory of God. Notice that my focus is not on leaders but leadership. Any member of a group can perform an act of leadership (from suggesting a course of action to complimenting a job well done). Designated leaders are not the only ones who help meet needs and goals. If they were, precious little would get done.

While leadership can be associated with *position* (president, coordinator, parent, teacher, pastor, treasurer and so on), in its essence it is a *function* (serving, initiating, planning, motivating, teaching and the like). While I cannot avoid the notion of position (nor will I try to), my focus will be on function. How are needs met? How are goals achieved? How do people grow in Christ? How can we help?

In the course of this book I will try to build the case that all of us can act as leaders in a group. Indeed I believe that encouraging this type of group leadership is the most effective way to foster growth. Thus one of the main tasks of designated leaders is to cultivate leadership in those being led. As I said, no matter who does these things, no matter what position they hold, whoever meets needs or goals for God's glory fulfills a leadership function. Though it may be a single act, it is an act of leadership.

James MacGregor Burns writes, "The test of leadership in all its forms . . . is the realization of purpose measured by popular needs manifested in social and human values."[1] What actually happened that helped people to fulfill their deepest longings? As Christians we also ask, What was done to allow people to become what God intended?

All this sounds galactic in proportions, something far beyond our abilities—and it is. Spiritual growth is a cosmic battle. "For we are not contending against flesh and blood, but against the principalities, against the powers, against the world rulers of this present darkness, against the spiritual hosts of wickedness in the heavenly places" (Eph 6:12). Spiritual growth is a mystery. "The kingdom of God is as if a man should scatter seed upon the ground, and should sleep and rise night and day, and the seed should sprout and grow, he knows not how" (Mk 4:26-27). Spiritual growth is God's work. "I planted, Apollos watered, but God gave the growth" (1 Cor 3:6).

Yet the spiritual welfare of others is something to which we can contribute in concrete ways. We contend. We scatter seed. We plant. We water. And we watch God bring the increase. God could have chosen many ways to save us and sanctify us. He could have offered instant Christlikeness and zapped us with grace. But he has chosen to bring about this miracle by working through frail, fallen humans like you and me.

How different is the world's view of leadership! Any success must be *our* success, not God's. We must be able to credit ourselves with any achievement. Why give God the honor when we did all the work? That is how the world views it. Unfortunately, if we are honest, that is also how Christians often view it. Now we rarely say it so baldly. Sneakiness has reached the level of high art among many Christians when it comes to such things.

You see, on the one hand, we say Christians are to be poor in spirit, humble in conduct and self-effacing in doing good for others. But, on the other hand, what qualities do we look for in our leaders? Our pastors should be (at least we want them to be) high-powered administrators, wealthy entrepreneurs spawning a variety of high-visibility ministries, or hyper-educated counselors with an armful of degrees and a knack for the media. Or better yet, all three in one. Such subtle and sincere sleight of hand is epitomized by the dear old woman who hoped a certain surgeon would become their pastor so that they could call their minister "Doctor."

From one side of our mouths we hail frugality, kindness and prayer while the other side simultaneously spouts the values of ostentation, big-name status and slickness of speech. We look to sports heroes or other celebrities who are new babes in Christ as spokesmen for Christ rather that to prayer warriors or faithful friends or mature men and women of the Word.

A Path to Travel

So in this book I have set out to present a Christian view of leadership—the scattering, planting and watering we do as God brings the growth. There are many, many books on leadership these days. Most, from what I have seen and read, focus on practicalities: how to get a job done, how to be effective, how to plan, how to use the right techniques, how to be a good manager. While these are worthwhile and while I too will share some practical ideas, I have chosen to make my emphasis pastoral rather than managerial. First, I have concentrated on people and on building character, God's character, into them. Second, I keep coming back to *our* character as we lead, more what kind of people we are to be than what activities we are to do. Often our character has as much influence on others as our actions.

This has been a scary adventure for me. I know better than anyone how my character falls short. I know my selfishness, how unwilling I am to serve. I know my anger. I know my impatience when growth is slow. And I feel inadequate to write a book like this. So please accept these words as those of one traveler to another and not as those of one who has arrived to those who have yet to start.

As I said before, leadership is not a *position,* a title, a static location on a map. It is possible to have a designated role of responsibility and yet exert little or no influence on others. Rather, leadership is a *function,* a process that moves and shifts from one person to another as the need and circumstance shift. But always it moves people, changes them, helps them to grow. It is a movement, a journey.

It is with the image of a journey that I have chosen to tie this book together. I see leadership as a path to travel. But it is not a single path with only one way to walk. Just as there are many ways to help the poor, to preach the good news and to grow in Christlikeness, so there are many ways to lead. Just as David, Moses, Hannah,

Jeremiah and Joseph were all different, so there are different paths of leadership.

Many people travel these roads. And I have written for all who have any spiritual responsibilities to others. This includes not only pastors and elders, Bible study leaders, Sunday-school teachers and prayer-group leaders, but also parents and other Christians who disciple, instruct and guide people toward growth in Christ. This is a broad group, for we are all involved in building up one another in Christ. So I have not limited myself to those with official, designated roles of leadership, but I have written to any the Holy Spirit might use to develop maturity in others.

Another unifying thread which binds the notion of Christian leadership together is the topic of the next chapter—servanthood. Christian leadership is a wide path of service containing many other subpaths which overlap and run parallel and intertwine with each other but which all move along the path of serving.

Chapter three discusses the path of following. Subsequent chapters consider other paths of service—facilitating, teaching, modeling and envisioning. There are other paths I could have chosen to discuss. My list is not exhaustive. But my hope is that these examples will help you to learn more of the open path of service that we all must travel. May the road rise to meet you.

2
The Path
of
Serving

*A Christian man is the most free lord of all, and subject to
none; a Christian man is the most dutiful servant of all,
and subject to everyone.*
Martin Luther

The New Testament lays its emphasis on leadership at the feet of
servanthood. Unfortunately, servants do not have the best of
images. How many murder mysteries end with "The butler did it"?
At the same time, how many heroes in the movies are waiters?
When we think of servants, our minds are filled with visions of long
faces, drab clothes, listless movements and passive demeanors.
What do these, we ask, have to do with the excitement of challeng-
ing, encouraging and guiding God's people? What is the Bible's
notion of servanthood, after all, and what does servanthood have
to do with leadership? Let me try to answer these questions by first

discussing whom we serve, second who we are and lastly what we are to do.

Whom Do You Serve?

A servant is, of course, one who serves. But whom or what do Christian leaders serve? Do we serve other people? Do we serve mankind? Do we serve Christians? Or do we serve a higher calling, a goal, a vision of a better world? Or do we, perhaps, if we are honest, serve ourselves?

Some say, indeed, that we can only serve ourselves—no matter what we do. In his best seller *Looking Out for Number One,* Robert Ringer writes,

All people act in their own self-interest *all* the time. . . . [Do I] believe Gandhi was acting selfishly when he sacrificed himself for the freedom of the Indian people? No, I can't say that I believe it. It would be more proper to say that I know it for a fact. I certainly was not a personal crony of Gandhi's, but I didn't have to be. I need only know that he was a human being and that the courses of action of all men, throughout history, have been chosen from the alternatives available to them at the time. Whatever Gandhi did, out of rational or irrational choice, he did because he chose to do it. If he acted in the hope of making millions of his countrymen happy, then that was the method he chose to seek his own happiness. It's only the means people choose to achieve their happiness which differ.[1]

If we can only act selfishly, then we should probably learn to be selfish as effectively as possible. That, of course, is what *Looking Out for Number One* so magnanimously offers to do for us at $9.95 plus tax. It almost sounds as though Ringer is competing for Calvinist-of-the-Year honors with such a thoroughgoing doctrine of total depravity. If even Mahatma Gandhi was completely selfish, what chance does a Scrooge like me have?

For more than one reason, however, Ringer will fall far short of Calvinist sainthood. Total depravity is an often misunderstood doctrine which does not mean that everything we do is utterly godless. No, it is possible, by God's common grace, for anyone to perform an honorable, self-giving act. Rather, total depravity means that the totality of creation has in some way been touched, tainted, twisted and perverted so that no thing or person remains wholly pure.

Haven't we all experienced this? I want to give Phyllis a birthday gift she will enjoy—a dinner together at a quiet restaurant. And soon I begin to think about how much I'll enjoy it.

Or I decide to help Tom shovel his driveway out of the latest blizzard that has dumped its winter wonderland on our doorsteps. After a while it occurs to me that now I won't mind so much asking Tom to help me when a big job comes up that I have to do.

Or Sue needs a ride home and I offer help, even though it's out of my way. Suddenly I am fighting the expectation that she should help me with the gas.

And here I am in the middle of writing a chapter on servanthood when I hear Phyllis upstairs struggling to get some tired, fussy children to bed. Will I stay at the desk in my highly protected state of creativity, or will I practice what I preach, get up from my desk of papers and help?

I decide to help.

That, in fact, is just the point. I will be pulled continually to act selfishly by a fallen nature that won't let go. Nevertheless, I am not forced to follow that inclination. I can choose to act differently. Even though such choice will be closely shadowed by selfish motives or partially unloving feelings, it is possible to be generous. We can truly give of ourselves. We do it all the time.

But why?

We are back to square one. Whom do we serve? Do we serve some ideal, some vision of the future? Franklin D. Roosevelt felt so. "The Presidency is . . . preeminently a place of moral leadership. All our great presidents were leaders of thought at times when certain historic ideas in the life of the nation had to be clarified."[2] Not many years ago we were hearing, "You are what you eat." Roosevelt says instead, "You are what you think." Someone who can help people think right will help them be right. Give us the right goal, the right ideal, the right knowledge, the right vision, and we will grow more harmonious and strong.

Let's face it, thinking right doesn't hurt. Truth, wherever it is found, ultimately has its source in God. The closer our thoughts are to his, the better. But a mechanical grasp of truth is insufficient. The demons believe (and correctly so) that there is a God. Yet it only makes them tremble (Jas 2:19).

This is the Jeffersonian fallacy. The better educated people are, the better people will be. Unfortunately, despite the high rates of literacy and the rapid dispersal of information through newspapers, books, radios and televisions, crime continues to rise, the arms race accelerates, and business has never been better for psychiatrists.

If serving a mere idea is insufficient, we come back to the question, Whom do we serve? Neighbors? Fellow Christians? The human race as a whole? To the lawyer who tested him, Jesus replied, "Be a neighbor to those in need that you meet, like the good Samaritan" (Lk 10:25-37). Later he told the apostles, "Love one another as I have loved you" (Jn 15:12). And Paul encouraged the Galatians, "Do good to all men" (Gal 6:10). So yes, we do serve our neighbors, our brothers and sisters in Christ, and humanity in general. But humanitarians do the same. People with no pretense of being Christian or holding to Christian principles are models of selflessness. We have already mentioned Mahatmah Gandhi. What makes Christian service different from his service?

Who Is Served?

In the openings to his letters to Rome, Galatia, Philippi and Titus, the apostle Paul introduces himself as a servant of Christ. His primary calling is to devote himself to the person of Jesus and to work to fulfill his Savior's priorities. His goal is to please Christ. "Am I now seeking the favor of men, or of God? Or am I trying to please men? If I were still pleasing men, I should not be a servant of Christ" (Gal 1:10). These are the questions servants of Christ ask themselves. Am I trying primarily to please God or others?

As leaders, then, our first question is not, Who am I to lead? But, Who am I led by? Who we lead, how we lead, and why we lead are all determined by who leads us. We don't begin with the problem or the task; we begin with the Taskmaster, the Lord of heaven.

When the disciples faced the hungry crowd of five thousand, they were overwhelmed by the problem. Their only solution was to send the people away. When Christ suggested that they feed the crowd, they again focused on the problem. "We have only five loaves here and two fish" (Mt 14:17). They failed to ask first, "Who is leading us?" They failed to consider that they were led by a person who healed lepers and cured paralyzed people, who forgave sin, who cast out demons, who taught with compelling authority, who calmed a raging storm with a word.

And isn't it the same with us? It is with me. When I wonder how I'll get all my work done, who I'll get to do a certain job, or how someone's hurt feelings will be healed, who I serve is far in the back of my mind. I forget I am led by a Savior who trampled death and overwhelmed the grave. I forget too that he has faithfully brought me through every previous crisis and problem I have faced. Instead, my current dilemma looms over me like a wave about to dash me on the rocks. Remembering that I am a servant of God calms my ocean of problems.

Am I discouraged because no one has my vision for helping the poor? I serve a God of hope. Am I afraid that I will fail to lead a good Bible study? I serve a God of peace. Am I too inadequate to counsel troubled friends? I serve a God of wisdom. Am I too insignificant to get humane treatment for prisoners? I serve a God of power.

Yet, not only are we helped when we are in trouble, we also have our priorities set for us by the character and work of the person we serve. Because we serve a holy God, we are to be holy. Because we serve a God of love, we are to love. Because we serve a God of truth, we are to speak truthfully. His character determines what our actions should be. Daniel wrote, "The people who know their God shall stand firm and take action" (Dan 11:32). Knowing who God is, we know how to act. Indeed, we are impelled and compelled to act. We are energized for God through his Spirit.

Knowing God changes more than our actions; it changes us. We become different people. We are in the process of being conformed more and more in our character and in our actions to the image of God. My point is that this process goes on only as we get to know God more and more. We cannot be active servants of God as he intended without knowing him. Continued devotion to prayer, to Bible study, to deeds of love and to words of truth will make us such people. Lord, may it be so.

Who We Are: Slaves of Christ
First, then, as servants we need to know *whom we serve*. Second, we need to know *who we are*. In the New Testament, the Revised Standard Version uses another word interchangeably with *servant—slave*. A slave is one who is owned by another, either permanently or for a period of time. For Christians this is more than an antiquated idea. It is a reality. "You are not your own," Paul tells us, "you were bought with a price" (1 Cor 6:19-20). We were once slaves to sin. Now we are slaves of God, bought with the blood of the Lamb. He owns us.

Here is another idea that makes servanthood unattractive. Indeed it makes all of Christianity unappealing. We live in an age of freedom. Unfettered choice is touted as an inalienable right. Who wants to limit his own freedom, much less dispense with it? But as God's people, we are not our own. When we became Christians, we accepted Christ's death for the one we deserved. In doing so, we gave up title to our own lives; the deed now belongs to Christ.

Certainly we can choose to disobey God and often do. That does not, however, change who owns us. Children can choose to disobey their parents. That does not, however, change their lineage. I don't mean that children are slaves. Rather, my point is that disobedience does not dissolve relationship.

Still we chafe at the idea. Slavery is an evil institution, degrading, disgusting, dehumanizing. Between one person and another this is so. But on a spiritual level, Paul tells us, this is the only kind of relationship that exists. "You who were once slaves of sin have become obedient from the heart, . . . and, having been set free from sin, have become slaves of righteousness" (Rom 6:17-18). Spiritually, freedom is fictitious We are slaves and only slaves. The only question is, Whose slave will we be? As Christians we have made a choice. Let us not turn our backs on that choice but go forward. "For just as you once yielded your members to impurity and to greater and greater iniquity, so now yield your members to righteousness for sanctification" (Rom 6:19).

His Children, His Friends

Our relationship with God is not one-dimensional, however. We are his slaves, true. We are also his children. Remarkably, the same act of redemption earned us both positions. In Galatians Paul writes, "When the time had fully come, God sent forth his Son, born of a woman, born under the law, to redeem those who were under the law, so that we might receive adoption as sons. . . . So through

God you are no longer a slave but a son, and if a son then an heir" (Gal 4:4-5, 7). At once we are made slaves of God and children of God who are heirs with free access to his infinite wealth and priceless fortune.

As J. I. Packer writes, "Justification is a *forensic* idea, conceived in terms of *law,* and viewing God as *judge.* . . . Adoption is a *family* idea, conceived in terms of *love,* and viewing God as *Father.*"[3] Adoption as children implies a deep, personal relationship with one who watches over and cares for us, who helps us to grow into full maturity. Such growth requires discipline. And a loving father will exercise authority in this way. But the aim is not to administer the mere punishment of a judge but to create a secure environment for change and growth.

We are also friends, which the Bible, interestingly enough, also contrasts with slavery. "You are my friends," Jesus told his disciples the night before he died, "if you do what I command you. No longer do I call you servants, for the servant does not know what his master is doing; but I have called you friends, for all that I have heard from my Father I have made known to you" (Jn 15:14-15). Just as Jesus informed the disciples of the most intimate details of his mission (including his suffering and death), God shares his plans and priorities with us. The whole of the Bible is God's intimate sharing with us as his friends. In particular, Ephesians 1 tells us he intends to unite all things in Christ. And Philippians 2 paints a graphic picture of at least part of his plan. "At the name of Jesus every knee [shall] bow, in heaven and on earth and under the earth" (Phil 2:10).

When you tell people your plans, you imply a trust in them. You don't expect that they will abuse the information you give them or that they will try to thwart your plans. Instead, you confide, hoping to gain an understanding ear or advice and perhaps support for your plans, support that is not coerced as from a slave but freely given as from a friend. Incredibly, such confidence implies a kind of equality between us and God. We can enter into his great work of eternity by his own offer.

Strong to Serve

From slave of God paid for in full, to a child of God adopted in love, to a friend of God offered a partnership—such is the range of relationships we have with God. What does all this have to do with leadership? Isn't this what all Christians are to have? What is unique about such relationships for those called to watch over others in Christ's body?

One answer is this: To serve others you must first know who you are. A servant and leader needs a strong self-image. Our identity is firmly tied to what we do. Ask someone, "Who are you?" and the answers you receive will often be responses to the question "What do you do?"

"I'm a truck driver."

"I'm an engineer."

"I'm a homemaker."

"I'm a farmer."

"I'm a student."

If we feel that what we do is insignificant, we will feel insignificant. Udo Middelmann tells how this is vividly portrayed at L'Abri in Switzerland. "Everyone who comes as a student is asked to help clean the lavatories. And it doesn't matter who comes. It is interesting to watch the reactions of various people. Those who really know who they are hardly mind at all, for they realize that cleaning the lavatory doesn't identify them. But a lot of people feel that they are identified by the work they do, so they resent the task, and that has sad results."[4]

Jesus had a firm grasp of who he was. In a classic passage on servanthood, we find the Last Supper about to begin. "Now before the feast of the Passover, when Jesus knew that his hour had come to depart out of this world to the Father, having loved his own who were in the world, he loved them to the end. And during the supper, when the devil had already put it into the heart of Judas Iscariot, Simon's son, to betray him, Jesus, knowing that the Father had given all things into his hands, and that he had come from God and was going to God, rose from supper, laid aside his garments, and girded himself with a towel. Then he poured water into a basin, and began to wash the disciples' feet, and to wipe them with the towel with which he was girded" (Jn 13:1-5).

The passage is rich, but I want to draw out just a few key points. First, notice what Jesus knew of himself. He knew "his hour had come." He was about to die an excruciating death which would fulfill the main purpose he had for coming to us as a man. *Jesus knew what he was to do.*

He also knew "that the Father had given all things into his hands." God was still sovereign. He was in control of a world that would soon seem to the disciples to be going completely berserk. Yet victory over death was already in hand. *Jesus knew who God was.*

Last, he knew "he had come from God and was going to God." Jesus was secure in knowing his origin and destiny as well as his present. He knew where he had been and where he was going. His identity was firmly implanted. *Jesus knew who he was.*

Yet why does John tell us these things now and in just this way? What does all this have to do with washing feet? John deliberately ties Jesus' strong self-image to an act of abject servanthood. So lowly is the act that Peter nearly refuses to allow Jesus to continue. "How could my Master do such a thing to me?" In fact, Jesus lowered himself even further in his ultimate act of service when he was raised on the cross. The certainty of who he was and of what his relationship with God was allowed him to fulfill his mission.

When we lack such certainty, such secure knowledge in who we are, our potential for leading rapidly diminishes. Once, just before a performance I was to sing in, the conductor left the choir in the hands of Jeffrey, an assistant, while she attended last-minute business. Jeffrey's job was to finish the warm-up and take the choir through some of the trouble spots. It was awful. A well-disciplined choir fell apart. No one listened to his instructions. Suggestions popped up here and there from the room. The accompanist started fouling up, not being used to Jeffrey's directions. I sat in great discomfort, embarrassed for him, anxiously hoping the choir would not be too disoriented when the concert began and the familiar wave of our conductor's baton once again greeted us.

Why did the choir suddenly collapse? Our leader was insecure. The choir immediately sensed it, and several people tried to fill the vacuum. Chaos resulted. Leadership requires some sense of ease and comfortableness with oneself, the task and others. Jesus' inner peace in the midst of terrible outward turmoil held the disciples together during that last Thursday meal. He could focus on their needs fully because of his firm knowledge of himself, his task and his God.

Before we go on, think again about whose feet he washed. The disciples'? Yes. But also Judas Iscariot's. Yet not just Judas, but Judas after "the devil had already put it into [his] heart . . . to betray him."

Who do you know who always seems to be working against you? You try to help here and he always seems to be there, too—ready to stop you! You have one idea of priorities, he has another. You start one project, and he uses the same limited resources to start a different one. If you don't have someone like this in your life now, you will have or you already have had or both. How to deal with them is always a problem. Jesus offered us a model. Wash his feet.

"No, not that," you say. "Be reasonable. You don't know Lynn. She's spiteful. Really. She gets pure pleasure from seeing me squirm. I mean, I could serve someone else's needs. But Lynn's?

What do I do? Play doormat to her football spikes?"

Doormat for Christ?

Are Christians doormats? Many people ask this. Are we wishy-washy pansies who bow down to the whims of every passing primate?

Let me state clearly and unequivocally, Christians are doormats. We are doormats for God. Evangelists often ask us to *surrender* our lives to God. This is not a bad image. We are at war with God, fighting for control of the territory of our lives. If we capitulate to him, he has absolute sway over us. We are his doormats. Jesus showed his utter submission to the Father's will in dying on the cross. Our obedience is to be just as complete.

Being a doormat for God, however, is very different from being a doormat for everyone else. It will not mean having the spine of a dishrag. In fact, it will mean the opposite. John 13 leaves no doubt about this. It took the clearest sense of identity, the firmest strength of character and the most determined sense of purpose for Jesus to wash the disciples' feet and then to die for them. (Indeed, let us not forget that Jesus also washed the feet of Peter, who denied his Lord not once but three times!) Such power and personal resolve are not found in doormats or dishrags. They are only found in servants, servants who know who they are. Jesus knew who he was, who God was and what he was to do.

Those who want to be leaders must then know who they are and must have a surer grasp than those they serve on what their relationship with God is like. Otherwise their service will be stunted.

Earlier I answered the question Whom do we serve? with the answer God. Of course, as I also said, we do indeed serve others. But the primary relationship of servants is with their master, not with those served. Servants are accountable to their masters (Mt 18: 26-34). Their success or failure is determined by their masters (Mt 24:45-50). Their status comes from their master (Jn 13:16;

15:20). They are motivated for the sake of their master (2 Cor 4:5). Their style of life is determined by who their master is. Finally, their master is the one they worship (Rev 19:5; 22:3).

The Priority of People

Whom do we serve? God. Who are we? Slaves, children, friends. Now we come to the last section of the chapter as I try to answer, What do we do? How do we serve? The answer lies in our important secondary relationship with others. The importance of this concern is emphasized by the first. The mission, the ministry that our master has given us, is people.

The importance of people is all too easy to miss in our age. What I really mean is that it's all too easy for *me* to miss. I've got a Bible study to lead, and I know it has to be over at noon. I'm all too ready to cut it off at noon just because that's what the schedule calls for, while ignoring what people may be learning or doubting or suffering, which may call for going overtime.

Likewise, a student I know from a wealthy family also proved quite capable of keeping the letter of the law while ignoring the spirit—that is to say, she ignored people. When she was unable to get others to help provide refreshments for their campus fellowship meeting, she simply rummaged around her home and found some stale crackers to bring. There was no sense of remembering who was being served, though in her mind at least, the job was done.

Jesus' run-ins with the Pharisees also point to the priority of people. In Luke 5:29—6:11, the Pharisees challenged Jesus on four different issues. Why do you eat with sinners (5:29-32)? Why do you eat instead of fast (5:33-39)? Why do you work on the sabbath? Why do you heal on the sabbath (6:1-5)? Through these questions we see their priority is outward righteousness while Christ's priority is people.

Jesus was more concerned for the well-being of sinners than

maintaining the appearance of righteousness by only eating with the respectable. And a mere rule about the sabbath must not take precedence over the people it was made for. Rather we should be allowed to celebrate in God's presence as wedding guests with the bridegroom. We are not relegated to the status of robotlike rule-followers but are elevated as honored guests. The priority is people.

The same theme is echoed throughout Christ's ministry. How often we read that he had compassion on the crowd (for example, Mt 14:13-14; Mk 6:34; 8:1-2)! Yet even with his great concern for the many, he always had time for just one. In Matthew 8:1-2 the crowds clamored for his attention, yet he gave it to a lowly leper. When an important philanthropist of the Jewish people needed help, Jesus still stopped to heal a ritually unclean woman (Mk 5: 21-43). On another occasion people crowded to hear him teach, but he gladly stopped to forgive and heal a paralyzed man. Jesus is the shepherd with the ninety-nine safe sheep who goes after the one that is lost (Mt 18:10-14).

Francis Schaeffer, the well-known Christian apologist, has many people clamoring for his attention. Yet he also has a well-earned reputation for giving himself to individuals of little consequence— as the world counts importance. During his years at L'Abri, his study center in Switzerland, his habit was to conduct a question-and-answer session where anyone could ask whatever he or she wished about Christianity. Each time Dr. Schaeffer would give a full answer, even if it took thirty minutes to do so. It didn't matter if the same question had been asked the night before or if the question was asked antagonistically. He still served them with the same full answer each time because, for Schaeffer, the person who asked it had God-given value and worth.

On one occasion, the film series *How Should We Then Live?* based on Schaeffer's book, was being shown. At one point in the films cans of different colored paint with holes punched in them swing from strings, dripping over a canvas. The crowd began to laugh at this attempt by modern people to create art. But afterward, Schaeffer took the crowd to task for their laughter. "You should be crying for these artists," he said. "It is tragic that human beings are trying to find meaning and significance in such ways." With the loss of God and his truth, our world seems to have lost itself as well.

People just don't seem to be worth much these days. The horror of the slaughter of six million Jews during World War 2 still sticks in our minds while we are barely aware of the fifty million people that are dying of starvation in the world. And millions of abortions in the United States, in Russia, in Japan and dozens of other countries each year also show how little we value human life. And this is civilization!

All this is discouraging, and well we might ask where to start. We begin with God. He then can give us the truth, the love, the values, the grace to go to our fellow human beings in a spirit of service.

The service he has given us is to meet the needs of others. That is Christian leadership. A leader, a servant, is someone who can identify the hurts, the concerns, the areas needing growth or strengthening in others and who then pours in healing and nourishment. Needs come in all varieties—spiritual, physical, emotional, intellectual, social, cultural. None is outside our area of concern. If we have caught God's priority for people, for whole people, we will look for all these needs.

"How shall we serve?" asks John Stott. "Evidently the Samaritan's service was determined by the man's need. . . . The one thing the Samaritan did not do was preach to him! He put oil and wine into his wounds, he did not stuff tracts into his pockets. . . . For who is my neighbor, whom I am to love? He is neither a bodyless soul nor a soulless body nor a private individual divorced from a social environment. God made man a physical, spiritual and social being. My neighbor is a body-soul-in-community. I cannot claim to love my neighbor if I'm really concerned for only one aspect of him, whether his soul or his body or his community."[5]

Leaders today need first to understand who their master is, second to fight the world's devaluation of human life, and third to resist the church's tendency to see only one aspect of human life as being worth attention. As we grow in these areas we will become servants as he intended.

What's the Difference?

A while back I asked, Aren't all Christians to behave this way? What is unique about Christian leaders? After all, they are no more and no less slaves, children and friends of God than are other Christians. I said then that Christian leaders are unique in having a strong sense of who they are as God's servants. What is unique about them beyond this? The answer is *nothing*. There is nothing else unique about us who serve by leading because all Christians are called to serve—to serve God, other Christians and the world.

Don't let the importance of this slip past you, however. This answer is far more important than the first. If we are all called to serve, then a leader does not serve alone. A leader does not do all the work alone, all the ministry alone or all the leading alone.

Some leaders have the impression that leadership is one among many gifts. This may be. But that doesn't mean that only a few will lead. Though there is a gift of evangelism, it doesn't mean only a few are called to evangelize. We all are. Likewise we are all called to lead, to stimulate others to grow in Christ. Some lead in faith, some in generosity, some in helps, some in administration, some in evangelism, some in prayer—but we all lead. A leader does not lead a group of Christians; the group itself must assume responsibility for its direction.

I often take on my shoulders responsibility for how my group is going. If it goes well, I pat myself on the back. If it goes poorly, I feel failure. But I am wrong to take either the credit or the blame. The group should. It is the group's responsibility.

It is difficult to take such an attitude because it means relinquishing power. And I like to be in control—or at least to think I am. I don't want to submit decisions to others. I want to make them myself. But my job is not to rule the local body of Christ in front of me. "Those who are supposed to rule over the Gentiles lord it over them, and their great men exercise authority over them. But it shall not be so among you; but whoever would be great among you must be your servant, and whoever would be first among you must be your servant, and whoever would be first among you must be slave of all. For the Son of man also came not to be served but to serve" (Mk 10:42-45).

This is our call.

3
The Path
of
Following

And when we think we lead we most are led.
Lord Byron

Frank was the sort of person you thought of as truly meek. He was a faithful churchgoer who dutifully followed the pastor's instructions about tithing or the instructions of the president of the men's club about how to help at the missions weekend or, for that matter, what almost anyone in authority told him about almost anything. One would have been tempted to call him passive, but he was quite conscientious in performing his assigned tasks.

Then came the fateful day that faithful Frank was asked to head a committee. He was promptly transformed into a dictator. He barked orders. He made demands. He expected compliance with his every plan. The metamorphosis was amazing. How did it happen? What turned this gentle person into an overnight Mussolini? Actually, nothing changed Frank. He was the same person before he headed the committee that he was afterward. He was the kind of leader he thought he should be, based on the kind of follower he was. Since he thought followers were to be the abject slaves of leaders, he also thought leaders were to be harsh taskmasters. So that's the kind of leader he decided to be. Since he had a twisted view of what it meant to be a follower, he had a twisted view of what it meant to be a leader.

Carolyn, a young Christian with a ravenous appetite for the Word, read through the entire Bible in the first nine months after her conversion, absorbing vast amounts along the way. Consequently, when she participated in a group Bible discussion, her comments would range from 1 Samuel to Romans to Job to Deuteronomy to Mark—even though the passage to be discussed was Psalm 19.

Carolyn's enthusiasm for the Word roused her interest in learning how to lead a group of people into discovering for themselves what was in a passage of Scripture. But when she led, what was intended to be a group discussion slowly became a one-woman lecture. She led the way she followed.

One of the key prerequisites for being a good leader is learning how to be a good follower. Aristotle put it this way, "He who has never learned to obey cannot be a good commander." Just as this was true for Frank and Carolyn, it is true in other settings. People who are ambitious and can't wait to get ahead are likely not to pay much attention to their subordinates. They have their attention bolted to what is in front of them (the next promotion) rather than to those behind them (the people they supervise). Likewise people who like to work independently of their bosses probably will have difficulty working with others because they expect them to operate the same way—independently. Our style of leading is often determined by our style of following.

Being a good follower can therefore help you to lead better. If we have learned to follow, then when we lead we know that we don't have to be alone in the process. I enjoy the challenge of leading a team of people or of developing a project on my own. But such responsibilities can also be burdensome. What if I goof? What if something goes wrong?

I find it refreshing to know that in these duties I am not alone. Being on the editorial staff of InterVarsity Press, I can go to my supervisor, work under him, put myself under his authority and realize I am not alone. Here is someone to help me. The burden is not totally mine. It is shared by someone else. This relieves me and strengthens me to lead those assigned to me and to finish the tasks I've been delegated. True, I do not have the power to do what I want as much as I might wish at times. But I do have great freedom to devote my energies to producing good books without the final weight of responsibility hanging around my neck. Because I am a follower, it is much easier to lead.

Following the Followers
Following is also important because we lead by following. Leaders follow God who has given us the task of following the needs of a certain group of people. One pastor I know decides what series of sermons he should preach by asking himself, "What are the needs of the people in my church?" By following their needs—spiritual, emotional, social, physical, intellectual—he discovers how to lead them. If they are chained to worries about the economy or about the threat of violence, he preaches on freedom in Christ. If they have difficulty keeping commitments and following through on projects, he preaches on steadfastness.

How can we identify needs in others and follow them? We identify needs in others by identifying with them as people. If we follow others to their point of need, they will see that we are on their side, that we care, that we understand—or at least that we are trying to. They will then be willing to follow us out of their need to the God who can meet their need.

Christ himself offers us this model to follow. For he is "not a high priest who is unable to sympathize with our weaknesses, but one who in every respect has been tempted as we are, yet without sinning. Let us then with confidence draw near to the throne of grace, that we may receive mercy and find grace to help in time of need" (Heb 4:15-16).

His temptation was no game, no pretense. It was real. He was tempted to commit idolatry. ("All these I will give you, if you will fall down and worship me," Mt 4:9.) He was tempted to disobey. ("Remove this cup from me," Mk 14:36.) He was tempted to despair. ("My God, my God, why hast thou forsaken me?" Mk 15:34.) His feelings were real. Isaiah 53:3-5 portrays a man who knows rejection, sorrow, grief and pain. He truly can sympathize with our weakness and struggle.

Jesus never turned away someone who had these temptations or these feelings. He identified with them at the risk of being accused of not obeying God himself.

Early in his ministry, many were drawn to him when they heard he could meet their needs for healing and exorcism. He didn't try to gather a great herd of followers. He didn't advertise or rent a stadium. People came at their own initiative because word got around that here was someone who could meet their needs. And, of course, as with the paralytic and his four friends, he offered more than they dreamed—forgiveness of sins.

His aim was not to draw a large crowd but to meet people at their point of need. And what was the result? Multitudes followed him. He followed them to their need. They followed him to the source of healing and strength and holiness.

Earl Wilson, a psychologist friend of mine, calls this "leaving your safe pad and going to the other person's safe pad." If you want to have an evangelistic Bible study, don't invite people to your place. Go to theirs. Leave your familiar territory and put yourself on theirs, meeting them on their own terms, in their own setting. By doing this faithfully, over a period of time, you can lead them to the One who can meet their needs.

While meeting needs is our calling, we are not called to meet all needs. We are finite human beings. God's will is that we be wise stewards of our bodies, time and energy. Most of us will be called to meet needs of a limited nature. Our family or our church or our college might be key areas of ministry. Hospitality, generosity, administration might be key gifts we are called on to use. But not all at once all the time. A need does not in itself constitute a call.

Despite the enormous spiritual and physical needs of first-century Palestine, even Jesus limited his ministry to three years, a few hundred square miles and a few thousand people. But he fully and strategically gave his life in obedience to God. We all need to ask God on what needs he wants us to focus our obedience.

Derived Authority
There is a final, crucial reason for learning to follow. No one ever stops being a follower. The leader is always responsible to someone else. In business, most leaders have bosses themselves whom they must follow. Such leaders with bosses are called middle managers. Rarely do leaders find themselves alone on the top of a pyramid. A corporate executive is responsible to the board of trustees. The board is responsible to the stockholders. A pastor reports to a bishop or to a congregation that can hire and fire him. A small group leader reports to a small group coordinator. Leaders always follow someone. If they don't, they are dictators and have ceased being leaders.

We are all perpetual followers because all authority is derived. Those with the power to do something invariably receive that power from someone else. No one leads autonomously. When the centurion came to Jesus requesting that his servant be healed, he stopped Jesus from actually coming to his house by saying, "Lord, I am not worthy to have you come under my roof; but only say the word, and my servant will be healed. For I am a man under authority, with soldiers under me; and I say to one, 'Go,' and he goes, and to another, 'Come,' and he comes, and to my slave, 'Do this,' and he does it" (Mt 8:8-9).

The centurian understood that his authority and power were not his own but were derived from another. This authority he could in turn pass on to others. Likewise the ultimate source of authority, God, could work through Jesus to command what should be done. So the centurion willingly submitted to him. Jesus was amazed at such faith and understanding and granted the centurion's request (Mt 8:10-13).

Of all the Gospels, John's makes it clearest that Jesus' authority was not his own.[1] Jesus came with his Father's agenda. "My food is to do the will of him who sent me, and to accomplish his work" (4:34). He came with his Father's authority. "I can do nothing on my own authority; as I hear, I judge; and my judgment is just, because I seek not my own will but the will of him who sent me" (5:30). He taught his Father's words. "I do nothing on my own authority but speak thus as the Father taught me" (8:28). He came on his Father's initiative. "I came not of my own accord, but he sent me" (8:42).

Jesus, just as the centurion suggested, also passed his authority on to others. He gave power to the disciples to exorcise, to heal and to teach (Lk 9:1-2). This transfer of authority was so complete that Jesus said, "He who receives any one whom I send receives me; and he who receives me receives him who sent me" (Jn 13:20).

In the Great Commission as well we see the pattern repeated: Jesus passes on his authority to others which he has received from the Father. "All authority in heaven and on earth has been given to me. Go therefore and make disciples of all nations, baptizing them in the name of the Father and of the Son and of the Holy Spirit, teaching them to observe all that I have commanded you" (Mt 28: 18-20). We are commissioned, not because we are so intelligent or strong or attractive or rich, but because Christ has all authority given to him and he has in turn given us authority to make disciples, baptizing and teaching all nations on his behalf.

Remembering the derivative nature of authority is a great antidote to pride. When Jesus was reluctant to answer Pilate's questions, Pilate said, "You will not speak to me? Do you not know that I have power to release you, and power to crucify you?" At this Jesus answered, "You would have no power over me unless it had been given you from above" (Jn 19:10-11). Pilate began by brandishing his power. But after Jesus spoke, he was reminded of his responsibility and tried harder to get Jesus released. He was not given free use of force when he was made procurator of Judea. He was accountable to others for his actions.

Moses: A Leader Who (Eventually) Followed

One of the great temptations leaders face is a feeling of not being dependent on anyone. The ability to say to one " 'Go' and he goes, and to another 'Come' and he comes' " creates the illusion that we are autonomous, responsible to no one, like the callous captain of a pirate ship. As Christians, however, we have made a declaration of dependence. We could not save ourselves apart from God's grace. We cannot sanctify ourselves apart from God's grace. We have deemed ourselves ultimately incompetent to run our lives and so have put ourselves under the authority of Another.

Moses faced this problem of dependence early in his career, long before he trembled before the burning bush. While he was still enjoying the privileges of an Egyptian prince, he somehow got the notion that he could be the deliverer of his people. One day, when Moses was forty (as Acts 7:23 tells us), "he went out to his people and looked on their burdens; and he saw an Egyptian beating a Hebrew, one of his people." So Moses took matters into his own hands and killed the Egyptian, hoping no one had seen him. "When he went out the next day, behold, two Hebrews were struggling together; and he said to the man that did the wrong, 'Why do you strike your fellow?' He answered, 'Who made you a prince and a judge over us? Do you mean to kill me as you killed the Egyptian?' " (Ex 2:11-14). Since his unauthorized execution was apparently known, Moses decided to flee Egypt.

The Hebrew's question to Moses was a good one. Who did make him prince and judge over the Hebrews? Had Pharaoh? Evidently not. Otherwise Moses would not have had to act covertly.

Had the Hebrews? Moses had been raised in an Egyptian palace, trained as an Egyptian prince, and only when he was grown did he go "out to his people and [look] on their burdens." They hardly knew Moses. Again the answer is no.

Had God made him a deliverer? The answer is crucial. Certainly God chose Moses to deliver his people from the oppression of the Egyptians. Moses, apparently, felt this calling. He was distressed by the suffering of his people. He wanted desperately to help, to do something to right the wrongs he saw. But he took matters into his own hands and impetuously killed the Egyptian. "He supposed that his brethren understood that God was giving them deliverance by his hand, but they did not understand" (Acts 7:25).

Here is the nub of the problem. He took matters into his own hands. *Even though he sensed his calling correctly,* he acted on his own authority. And he was wrong. He could possibly have ruined God's plan and purpose for his life. It cost his people another forty years of suffering while God worked to remake Moses into the right kind of deliverer.

Moses' plight should be a sharp reminder to us all. We are so anxious to discover our gifts, to discern how God is calling us, to receive God's guidance for our lives. The world is an uncertain path in a dark forest, and we strain to see any light to direct our steps. Breaking into a sprint at the first glimmer in the night will only bring our noses into quick contact with the ground. Instead we must walk cautiously, keeping our eyes diligently fixed on the light, feeling each step carefully till we have found our way out.

Having glimpsed the light, having sensed God's call, is not the end of the journey. We must then continue to walk faithfully, following God to see how and when and where and with whom we should use our gifts.

By the time Moses came across the burning bush, his years of hardship in the desert had made him a very different prince. Though God told him directly, "Come, I will send you to Pharaoh that you may bring forth my people, the sons of Israel, out of Egypt," Moses replied, "Who am I that I should go to Pharaoh?" (Ex 3:10-11). Where is the presumptuous prince? Having been so humiliated by his failure to carry out his call correctly, by his exile from the court of Pharaoh and by his lowly duties as a shepherd, Moses was ready to be built back into the kind of leader God intended.

By chapter 4, Moses has begun to learn how to follow. While in Exodus 3 he took matters into his own hands, in Exodus 4 he asks permission of his father-in-law to leave to go to Egypt. He has put himself under Jethro's authority and so is allowed to go with his blessing (4:18).

Though we see Moses continually giving commands in the rest of Exodus, they are at the Lord's direction. At God's word he commanded Pharaoh to let Israel go (5:1, 3; 8:1). Likewise he commanded Aaron to bring certain plagues (7:19; 8:5-6, 16-17). The people of Israel were also commanded by Moses at God's word (34: 32; 39:32, 42).

The fruits of Moses' newfound followership (and that of the people of Israel) became stunningly clear. "Thus did all the people of Israel; as the LORD commanded Moses and Aaron [to have Passover], so they did. And on that very day the LORD brought the people of Israel out of the land of Egypt by their hosts" (Ex 12:50-51).

The Consent of the Governed

The derivative nature of authority makes it clear that we are responsible to someone above us. But it does more. It profoundly affects our understanding of how we relate to those we serve. Rather than giving us the power to impose our will on others like the "Gentiles . . . and their great men [who] exercise authority" (Mt 20:25), our authority extends only over those who choose to place themselves under it.

To some this can be a frustrating problem. "How can I get Mary to help make posters if being coordinator doesn't mean anything?" "What is a husband if he can't have the final say?" "How is a pastor supposed to lead his flock if no one is obligated to follow?"

Because our authority does not lie in ourselves, we cannot require anyone to obey. Instead, others must voluntarily choose to place themselves under our authority as a result of God's work in their lives. As Howard Butt says, "Leadership is a gift from people under you."[2]

This is true in a Christian fellowship as much as it is in a Christian business or mission organization, or in General Motors for that matter. If people don't want to be led, they won't be. Recalcitrant employees can buck their boss, who can retaliate by cutting their pay or putting them on the night shift or making them do the lowest level work. But that won't necessarily bring about the desired reform. And even if their boss should fire them, that wouldn't make him or her the leader of such rebels. It would only formalize the fact that the supervisor is not their boss. Once off the payroll, their ties would be totally severed.

In Ephesians 5 Paul never commands husbands to make wives obey. Rather the obedience of wives to their husbands is a matter solely between wives and the Lord. The husbands' role is to sacrifice themselves for their wives as Christ sacrificed himself for the spiritual welfare of his bride, the church. Christ never forced any individual or group to obey. No one was kidnaped into the kingdom. Instead Christ "loved ... gave himself up ... nourishes ... cherishes," in order that his bride might be sanctified and cleansed. This is what husbands are to do.

Christ died for the church. I can certainly give up a golf game to go on a picnic with my wife, or sacrifice sleep with a crying baby so that she can be alert enough for a quiet time in the morning, or put down the newspaper to talk over the not-so-spectacular events of the day. In response to such acts and such an attitude on my part, she will likely on her own choose to follow my lead.

But I do not nurture her only to gain obedience. I seek to nurture her whether or not she chooses to be subject. Christ sacrificed himself even while his bride betrayed him. Judas sold him. Peter denied him. The rest fled from him. And two thousand years of church history is full of subsequent acts of disobedience. Still he sacrificed—while we were yet sinners.

Pastors, parents, small group leaders—all face similar situations. Obedience can be coerced. But such obedience does nothing to foster spiritual growth. Like the child made to sit in the corner who says, "I'm standing up on the inside," those coerced into obedience may also be rebelling inside.

How are authority and freedom balanced? Mark, a Christian leader, says his authority extends over those who will listen to him. He will be very straight and, when necessary, severe with such people. He will not avoid the hard demands of the Christian life but speak plainly.

Other members of his Christian fellowship, however, are not prepared or choose not to place themselves under his spiritual leadership. With such people he is polite and courteous and makes no demands of discipleship on them. He knows they are not ready to listen. So he saves himself from frustration and from a reputation as a domineering leader by making himself available to them but waiting for them to first choose to submit.

As Christ said to the Jews who demanded that he reveal himself, "You do not believe, because you do not belong to my sheep. My sheep hear my voice, and I know them, and they follow me" (Jn 10: 26-27). He exercises authority over the sheep who listen. Those who refuse to listen are not under his authority, and he does not lead them.

This is all the more remarkable coming from someone whose authority is evident. In Luke's Gospel, for example, we see his authority in teaching (4:31-32), in casting out demons (4:35-36), in healing (4:38-39), in forgiving sins (5:20-26), in ruling nature (8:25) and in subduing the power of death (8:49-55). Nonetheless, those who choose not to follow him are allowed to go their way, as did the rich ruler (18:18-23).

Likewise we cannot require submission, we husbands or parents or pastors or Sunday-school teachers or Christian workers of any kind. We can only wait, pray, be available and then lead those who choose to follow.

Our authority is not our own to wield. It belongs to another. We must therefore be great in service (Mt 20:26).

The Character of the Follower
If the kind of leader we are flows from the kind of follower we are, if the burden of leading is eased when we also follow another, if the

very act of leading is one of following the needs of others, and if we will always be followers since all authority comes from outside ourselves, then we had better be about the business of learning how to follow as much as of learning how to lead. What are the characteristics of a follower? I would like briefly to address three.

First, a follower is one who *listens*. We just read about Jesus, who said, "I am the good shepherd; I know my own and my own know me. ... They will heed my voice" (Jn 10:14, 16). His sheep hear his voice, but they hear in the Jewish sense of *hear*. Hearing is also heeding. Listening is not merely allowing sound waves to vibrate our ear drums. To truly listen means to internalize what is said and then to respond. "Let every man be quick to hear," James says. "But be doers of the word, and not hearers only, deceiving yourselves" (1:19, 22). We are kidding ourselves, lying to ourselves, if we think that merely absorbing God's Word is enough. The act of hearing is not complete until we have lived his Word as well.

Many of us read the Bible, study the Bible, go to conferences on the Bible and talk about the Bible. But as Thom Hopler has said, we who know the Bible so well are in grave danger, for as James says, "Whoever knows what is right to do and fails to do it, for him it is sin" (4:17). Hopler has further suggested that perhaps it is time to stop learning about the Word and start doing what has been lying dormant in our minds.

The Bible says, "If your brother sins against you, go and tell him his fault, between you and him alone" (Mt 18:15). We know it. We believe it. Do we do it? Too rarely. It is excruciatingly difficult to confront someone. We don't believe doing so will provide an avenue of healing. We can only see the anguish of the act. We have failed to listen.

The Bible says, "I do not mean that others should be eased and you burdened, but that as a matter of equality your abundance at the present time should supply their want" (2 Cor 8:13-14). But that new video-tape player is so inviting, and that camera will never be at a lower price, and those clothes are so much in style, and I can't live without my own washer and drier or my week in the Rockies or those new albums. And so those in want continue in want, and I continue in abundance. I have failed to listen.

God never said listening would be easy. It takes concentration, openness and the will to respond. If we are to follow our Lord, we must first hear his call, "Follow me."

Second, a follower is one who *suffers loss*. In Luke 9:57-62 three would-be disciples are confronted with the issue of following. The first says he will follow Christ anywhere, but the Lord tells him he has no place that is truly home. A follower faces the loss of home too. The next one wanted to bury his father and no doubt to collect his inheritance. But he was told that a follower has higher priorities. The last man asks to say good-by first to those at home. But a follower is to have no second thoughts. One must be single-minded in following.

Jesus himself paid the same price. He learned to follow at great cost. "Although he was a Son, he learned obedience through what he suffered" (Heb 5:8). The results of his suffering in his following are staggering. "Being made perfect he became the source of eternal salvation to all who obey him" (Heb 5:9).

Henri Nouwen writes, "Who can save a child from a burning house without taking the risk of being hurt by the flames? Who can listen to a story of loneliness and despair without taking the risk of experiencing similar pains in his own heart or even losing his precious peace of mind? In short: 'Who can take away suffering without entering it?' . . . So long as we define leadership in terms of preventing or establishing precedents, or in terms of being responsible for some kind of abstract 'general good,' we have forgotten that no God can save us except a suffering God, and that no man can lead his people except the man who is crushed by its sins."[3]

Christ does not ask us to pay a price he has not paid, nor to go where he has not gone. We follow a suffering God.

Third, a follower is one who *aggressively submits*. As followers, of course, we obey another. As Christians our allegiance is to the Lord. But such submission is not turning off our brain, putting our life in neutral and coasting to heaven. Our submission is active; it is determined; it is aggressive. The apostles submitted vigorously to their risen Lord by carrying the good news to Africa, Asia and Europe in the face of fierce opposition. As for our Lord himself, "When the days drew near for him to be received up, he set his face to go to Jerusalem" (Lk 9:51). He was determined to carry out this act of aggressive obedience to his Father.

So often our view of submission fosters a dishrag mentality. But when Paul told husbands and wives to "be subject to one another out of reverence for Christ" (Eph 5:21), he didn't promise a life of quiet passivity for either party. He compared wives to Christ's church which was to conquer the world with his love—not exactly a rocking-chair activity. He said husbands were to be like Christ who died to sanctify the church—not a matter of merely giving her flowers for her birthday. Christ gave his church "all authority" in its role of obedience. Our submission carries with it nothing less. Let us never fool ourselves or anyone else into thinking that following Christ (or any other form of submission in Christianity) calls for anything less than our fullest potential, our best efforts and our most vigorous determination to obey.

Leading Together
The intimate relation between leading and following means it is impossible to truly lead as a "one-man show." Indeed, if it is true that leaders will always be followers, it is also true that followers will always lead.

Once I was leading a group and needed to shift some responsibilities. So I presented my plan to each person individually. But after the changes were made, I detected some dissatisfaction. There was unhappiness at not being consulted beforehand and at having a decision imposed. The disharmony that resulted affected the work everyone was doing.

Because the group was not allowed to lead by freely expressing their views, they took the lead by expressing their dissatisfaction in a variety of direct and indirect ways. I did not realize that followers will always lead. I had circumvented their input into the decision-making process only to be blocked myself.

Take another example. "A janitor enters the office of a university president after normal working hours to clean up. The president is still at his desk working on papers. As quietly and unobtrusively as possible, the janitor sweeps, dusts, and empties ashtrays. But after a time the janitor decides he must disturb the president to sweep under his desk. He coughs, gets the president's attention, and asks the president to slide his chair back. The president slides his chair back—at the janitor's direction—and the janitor finishes up his service!"[4]

The point of these illustrations is not that the leaders exerted no influence and that the followers exerted all the influence. No, in both cases authority flowed from the leader (me and the president) to those under him (the group and the janitor). And since those followers also had authority, the leaders were bound to respect it.

What I am describing is cooperation, teamwork, community, working together. Leadership is a function of the whole body. Sometimes the hand stretched out in front in a dark room tells the whole body to stop when it touches a wall. Sometimes the ear tells the whole body to turn around when it hears a noise. Certainly the brain processes the information sent by the hand and the ear, but if the brain refused to listen and only followed its own counsel, the body's nose might be broken when it contacted the wall. Leadership is a corporate act of following.

4
The Path
of
Facilitating

I would rather set ten men to work than do the work of ten men.
Dwight L. Moody

It was a little embarrassing. If people had asked me what I was read-ing and left it at that, it would have been fine. But, unfortunately, after I told them *Watership Down,* most went on to ask, "What's it about?" I tell you, it's not easy telling people you're reading a 400-page story about rabbits. But I was. And it wasn't too long afterward that I was thoroughly enthralled with it and began telling people about it who didn't even ask.

The story opens with Hazel and Fiver, two brothers who live to-gether in a warren. A terrible feeling of danger comes over Fiver one day that Hazel tries to ignore. But the sense of dread continues, and Fiver urges Hazel to make all the rabbits leave the warren. Although dubious, Hazel decides to go to the Chief Rabbit because of Fiver's intensity and because similar premonitions of danger that Fiver had had always proved true.

The Chief Rabbit refuses to listen, but the two brothers manage to assemble a small group who believe the danger is real. Before they can leave, however, they are stopped by the Chief Rabbit's soldiers. Bigwig, a discontented soldier who has joined those leaving, attacks his former comrades, and the others help Bigwig fight off the soldiers. So Hazel and the rest escape, making their way into the night.

They travel some distance and Bigwig suggests they rest. After surveying the tired, fearful group, Hazel says, " 'Yes, all right, we'll rest here. . . . Come on, Dandelion, tell us a story. I know you're handy that way. Pipkin here can't wait to hear it.' Dandelion looked at Pipkin and realized what it was that Hazel was asking him to do. Choking back his own fear, . . . he began."[1] The story calms them all so that they can continue their journey.

They come to a river and are forced to cross it when a dog approaches. Pipkin and Fiver, however, are too weakened to make the swim. Suddenly Blackberry realizes the two could sit on a board and float across while the rest swim. Though Hazel doesn't understand what Blackberry means, Fiver does. So once more the group escapes with all intact.

Crows, thorns, a road with cars and trucks, rabbit snares, a barn full of rats, long days and nights above ground, all threaten them as they travel on. The dangers, the exhaustion, the fear, the frayed nerves make petty fights and arguments frequent. But soon, "there was no more quarreling. . . . They had come closer together, relying on and valuing each other's capacities. They knew now that it was on these and on nothing else that their lives depended."[2] The life of even the biggest depends on that of the smallest. When Bigwig is caught in a snare, it is Pipkin's and Fiver's small heads that can reach in the hole the others had dug to bite through the wood peg anchoring the deadly wire.

Eventually they come to the safe, high, dry down of Watership and begin to dig a fine large warren of their own under the direction of Strawberry. Hazel, to the bewilderment of the others, also makes friends with a mouse and a wounded seagull, Kehaar. But this strange, feathered companion proves invaluable in solving a problem so obvious everyone had missed it—everyone, that is, but Hazel. They were all male rabbits. "We have no does—not one—and no does means no kittens and in a few years no warren."[3] Once Kehaar is able to fly again, he consents to look over the nearby territory for another warren where Hazel and the others can go to find some females to balance their all-male troupe.

The rest of *Watership Down* is the exciting story of how the gifts of each one are used to overcome this last obstacle to establishing a new warren. It is just these dynamics that I want to consider in this chapter. While I wish I could dwell on the most dramatic episodes of the story or on the most intriguing characterizations, I have tried to emphasize how Richard Adams's book is a delightful and entertaining study of the ways a facilitator can bring out the best in others and achieve far more than one could by trying to be a superstar or a dictator.[4]

Hazel was not threatened by Bigwig's strength or Blackberry's wits or Fiver's insight or Strawberry's ability to dig or Kehaar's to fly or Dandelion's to tell stories. Each one was better than Hazel in his specialty. Hazel had the ability to mold these diverse personalities and talents into a united team—encouraging, suggesting, listening, risking. He offers a model of how a leader can and should be a facilitator of other people's strengths. The whole book is worth studying and discussing on this point alone—perhaps even by your leadership team.

Bring Out the Best

What is a facilitator? Perhaps you've heard the commercial for Hellmann's mayonnaise. "Bring out the Hellmann's . . . bring out the best!" The pun is apt. While claiming to be the best mayonnaise, Hellmann's suggests that it brings out the best flavors in other foods.

This is certainly true for my taste buds. One of the reasons I like Thanksgiving so much is the leftovers. Cold turkey sandwiches are a delight. The problem is that what I like best is the white meat, which tends to be a little dry. But a generous supply of mayonnaise enhances the flavor of the turkey, the crunch of the lettuce and the texture of the toast. The mayonnaise itself is almost forgotten for the strength of the rest. But without the mayonnaise, it is an unhappy affair. With it, there are few meals (or snacks) I like better.

Facilitators are people who bring out the best in others. They are able to draw out the strengths in people without drawing attention to themselves. Like the mayonnaise, they may not be noticed. But without facilitators, nothing is as good.

When Hazel and his friends encountered an unfriendly warren in *Watership Down,* the enemy rabbits didn't realize Hazel was the Chief Rabbit even when they met him. They thought the big, strong Bigwig was the Chief Rabbit. They saw Bigwig as a courageous, daring and tenacious fighter. At one point in the final battle they ask Bigwig why he doesn't give up.

"My Chief Rabbit has told me to defend this run and until he says otherwise I shall stay here."

"His Chief Rabbit?" said Vervain, staring.

It had never occurred to [them that Bigwig] was not the Chief Rabbit of his warren. Yet what he said carried immediate conviction. He was speaking the truth. And if he was not the Chief Rabbit, then somewhere close by there must be another stronger rabbit who was.[5]

In fact, of course, Hazel was not nearly as strong physically as Bigwig. He had even been wounded once by a gun and had a noticeable limp. But no one brought out the best in others the way Hazel did.

This seems to me to be what Ephesians 5, a passage I've already mentioned, is getting at in calling husbands to model their spiritual leadership on that of Christ. "Husbands, love your wives, as Christ loved the church and gave himself up for her, that he might sanctify her, having cleansed her by the washing of water with the word, that he might present the church to himself in splendor, without spot or wrinkle or any such thing, that she might be holy and without blemish" (Eph 5:25-27). As Christ brings out the best in the church, so husbands are to bring out the best in their wives. They are not to fear or be threatened by them, but to work to help them become all God intends.

Phyllis delights in raising children. Even though a second income would be nice, we do without so that she can focus her attention on Stephen, Susan and Philip. Yet Phyllis also gets tremendous satisfaction from writing. So when she has an article in mind, I adjust my schedule as needed to make sure that she has the blocks of uninterrupted time that are necessary to write. My goal—our goal—is that she develop all the different gifts God has given her.

Phyllis, by my own estimation, is far more personal than I am. She could strike up a conversation with a tree stump and get the stump to do most of the talking. So I try to foster her gifts of hospitality and counseling and discipleship, encouraging her to spend time with those who need listening ears and sound words.

I could easily be threatened by her gregarious nature and winning ways, wondering if anyone appreciates me as much as they do her. But I have always felt (well, almost always) that the stronger she is, the stronger I am. Her social ease rubs off two ways: I learn from her, and others perceive both of us to be like her in this way, even though I have much to learn.

A facilitator, then, is like a midwife. The mother and the child get the deserved glory, for they have done the labor. But the midwife is there to ease the process, to assist as needed, to encourage when it seems the baby will never come.

As is true with most leadership roles, you don't have to be a person "in authority" with a big (or even a small) title to be a facilitator. Anyone can do it, almost anywhere.

"Bill, when are you going to join the choir? They can always use basses as good as you."

"Sue, did you ever think of putting your business sense to work as our treasurer?"

"You have such a heart for the world hunger problem, Henry. What could you do to help the rest of us understand what's going on?"

"Your prayer at last night's meeting sure moved me, Jill. It got me to praying all day."

"Why don't you let me handle the administrative part of the retreat so you can focus your time on the program? You're better at that than anyone else, and you don't have enough time to do both."

Every member of the body can exercise leadership by facilitating. If only "the leader" did this, precious little would get done. But as each one *appreciates, initiates, cultivates, delegates* and *supplicates,* the best is brought out in each other. Let's look at each of these forms of facilitation more closely.

Appreciate: Praise Thy Neighbor

The simplest way to bring out the best in others is to tell them that you appreciate what is already good about who they are and what they do. A regular dose of honest affirmation can transform a person. I've seen it happen many times. One day at lunch I made a point twice of telling Stephanie, a friend known for being, shall we say, feisty, that I had appreciated all that she had done and how well her work reflected on the whole group. She was a different person all afternoon. On another occasion, a rather reluctant helper instantaneously became my best ally after I honestly expressed my thanks for a job well done.

Praise has mysterious powers. I have watched how the use and abuse of affirmation has tilted the outcome of more than one volleyball game. Those teams which focus on the good plays their members make and don't step in to take away shots from each other find themselves on top of more talented teams who carp and complain and criticize each other at every flub, major and minor.

The point is not to manipulate people into being nice by telling them good things that aren't true. That will, in fact, backfire in the long run. People have a sense of what is good about them. They know when you are patronizing them. They may not be able to articulate their perception, but they feel it in their gut.

When I was young I always hated it when people said to me, "Well, haven't you become quite a little man!" Yuck! I knew I wasn't a man yet. I was only six. And I didn't like being called little either, because I knew I was growing some. While outwardly it might have sounded like a compliment, it made me feel like someone had put syrup on my hands and I couldn't wash it off. People who said such things made no friends with me.

While praising is the simplest way to facilitate, the simplest way to praise is to comment on what someone has done. For those of us who aren't very comfortable with affirming people, we can start by thanking them for their efforts to arrange for a speaker or for being so faithful in coming to the Bible study or for keeping the place so clean. Inevitably, a regular diet of such comments will mean harder work next time to get a good speaker, continued good attendance and a cleaner place.

Beyond this, however, we must also show appreciation for who people are, for their character.

"Thanks for being so cheerful."
"I've always appreciated your stick-to-itiveness."
"Your patience is amazing!"
There are also ways to show appreciation besides say it. Putting it in writing in a note or card can make the comment even more concrete. Patti sat down each Monday to write a note of appreciation to her pastor for the Sunday service. She knew he would hear enough negative comments about various aspects of church life throughout the week that he would need something positive. She was bringing out the best in her spiritual leader.

Small gifts can also do the same and can be a great alternative for those who aren't comfortable with words.

As often as not, however, it's not the words we are uncomfortable with, it's the praise. We don't feel easy about saying such things. John Powell writes,

When I hear something complimentary about another, why do I say: "Don't tell him. It might go to his head"? Why do I not want others to be happy with themselves? I don't want "it" to go to his head. What is "it" that I don't want in the head of my brother or sister? What *do* I want in his head? If another rejoices in some success, why do I immediately accuse him of bragging? Why have I become such a jealous guardian of his humility? Why does it concern me so much?

Perhaps the answer to these and similar questions will lead me to the realization that I do not want him to love himself because I am unable to love myself. . . . If I cannot openly and honestly acknowledge my own strengths and assets, I will not want anyone else to acknowledge his.[6]

For many of us, our own insecurity makes us reluctant to show appreciation. We are so concerned with ourselves and how we stack up against others that we resist the idea of praising someone else. We don't want to admit that another might be a better organizer or speaker or host or helper or counselor or Bible study leader than we are. My worth is threatened in my own eyes and possibly in the eyes of others. "If I affirm Ted, he might be encouraged to lead more Bible studies. And if he does, others will see how good he is and want him to lead instead of me."

All of us have problems with self-esteem that make it difficult to compliment others. But we imagine that highly visible leaders do not. Surely, we think, they are so self-assured and confident that they have no problem in this way. Yet this is not true. Their insecurity, in fact, tends to make them put more and more distance between them and the rest of the group.

On the other hand, there are a few leaders who, while needing affirmation, require less of it than most. Their self-esteem is lifted by simply knowing they have done a good job. They tend to assume that others are like them and also need little affirmation; consequently, they give little. They pay little attention to the concerns of others and bury themselves in their work, their source of esteem.

Both these extremes—the insecure, distant leader and the task-oriented leader—result in the same behavior: no affirming of others. They also arise from the same cause: self-concern. The first group continually compare themselves with others, wondering how they are coming across. They have little time to consider the needs of others. The second group continually focus on their jobs and how to do them better. They have little time to consider the needs of others.

Such self-concern is a knotty problem. How can I esteem others until I am esteemed? Yet how can others esteem me until I esteem them? Someone needs to break in from the outside to stop this ever-accelerating circle of me-ism. That, of course, is what Jesus Christ has done. Forgetting self, he sacrificed himself for us, sinners though we are, and invested us with great worth and dignity. Our very beings are secure in him. We need not earn our value. We need not fear looking less important than others. To do so is to deny the worth of what Jesus has done and ultimately to mock his death.

We are, therefore, free to bring out the best in people, forgetting self and focusing on others, appreciating the people God has made them to be and saved them to be.

Initiate: Giving It Not Taking It

The idea of initiating is one that commonly floats in our conscious and unconscious minds when we think about leaders. Leaders are starters. They introduce ideas. They make the first move. They bring up topics, problems, concerns, hopes. They make plans.

While these are certainly true of initiators, two other factors dull this stereotype. First, as with appreciating, you need not be a designated leader to initiate. Anyone can do it. Once at a restaurant, after being served, everyone in our group was waiting rather awkwardly before beginning when Bill said, "Tom, why don't you give thanks for us?" Everyone breathed easily as Tom prayed, and then we ate. Bill was not the designated leader of the group, but he filled the leadership role of facilitator by initiating prayer. It was a simple question, but it was an act of leadership nonetheless. Asking questions is one way all of us initiate. They can be simple or profound.

"Did you ever think of beginning Sunday worship with announcements?"

"Why do we evangelize as we do?"

"Could we add fifteen minutes to the conference schedule to give people more time to pack?"

An initiator may also undertake some duty without being asked: passing out songbooks before the meeting starts, collecting money for a needy family, organizing a basketball game. As we initiate anything, however, it is important to remember our goal is to bring out the best in others. How can we meet the needs of others and help them grow? Passing out hymnals ahead of time may keep this from being a distraction during the meeting itself so that people can concentrate on what God wants them to learn. Collecting money can help many people to grow in generosity while meeting a physical need. Basketball can meet another kind of physical need or a need for fellowship.

This brings us to the second way Christian initiating breaks our common notions of leaders as highly motivated self-starters. We often say Martin *took* the initiative, as if he were grabbing it away from someone else. But initiating, like the other ways we can facilitate, is something we give to those we serve to meet their needs. We don't wait till someone asks us to serve them; we look for such opportunities.

A good initiator is like a good waiter. He comes to your table, introduces himself courteously and makes you feel welcome. He then leaves you alone to choose your meal. But he will not keep you waiting too long to order. If you have questions, he'll be glad to answer them. If your water glass is low, he'll fill it. If the waiter does his job, you will not have to initiate a conversation with him once during the meal. You won't have to remind him to take your plates or to bring the check. He will have anticipated your needs each time. Such initiative is always for your good and is given openly, without grudging.

We are all called to be such servants, searching for ways to help others become more like Christ. Sometimes taking initiative in this way is not as much fun as getting a basketball game together. As I mentioned before, confronting a fellow believer with sin is one such case. "If your brother sins against you, go . . ." (Mt 18:15). The lack of such initiative in the church today has made us soft on sin. As the world seems to become more and more self-centered and corrupt, and yesterday's vices become today's fashions, the church also loses its perspective on what is and isn't sinful. We need more people— not just pastors and counselors but concerned, committed, courageous Christians—to be willing to confront lovingly and honestly those who have chosen to disregard God's law.

Initiating also affects the other side of sin—our own. "If you are offering your gift at the altar and there remember that your brother has something against you, leave your gift there before the altar and go; first be reconciled to your brother, and then come and offer your gift" (Mt 5:23-24). Much inertia resists such initiation. It is easier to ignore our sin or to rationalize it than to confront it. But if we are more concerned about God and his holiness in us than about admitting a wrong to another and asking forgiveness, we will *give* the initiative for reconciliation.

Cultivate: Gifts for All
Facilitators not only appreciate and initiate, they also cultivate. In 1 Corinthians 12 Paul compares the church to a body. "The body does not consist of one member but of many. . . . If the whole body were an eye, where would be the hearing? If the whole body were an ear, where would be the sense of smell? But as it is, God arranged the organs in the body, each one of them, as he chose. If all were a single organ, where would the body be?" (1 Cor 12:14, 17-19). Leaders who make themselves the highly visible, ultimate arbiters of all disputes and chief architects of all plans are leaders who are building churches that are "single organs." Imagine a six-foot ear or a one-hundred-and-seventy-pound eyeball. Monstrosities! Organizations that are built on the preaching, teaching, thinking, entertaining, fund-raising charisma of one person—of which there are many in Christendom—are built contrary to Scripture. These are not bodies. These are grotesque mutations.

Yet many Christian leaders believe they must chair every meeting, speak at every function, plan every event, oversee every operation and make every decision. Because no one can do all that, they will be hindered from achieving their larger goals, whether to evangelize or to comfort or to grow or to help the needy. To achieve such goals for a fellowship or a church or a school or a family or a city or a country, the best efforts of many people are essential. Yet so many leaders fail to cultivate the gifts of others. Why? Because they are afraid.

They fear the job will not be done as well by someone else. They've had years of experience learning how to do it best. Why let someone who has had no training organize the evangelism committee?

They also fear, however, that someone else may indeed do a better job. And if others find out, their position will be threatened. So when any others who are especially talented or bright or productive come along, they are only able to use their strengths until they hit the limits of their leader's insecurities. Then they either stagnate or leave in frustration. The result? The work suffers because good people have been lost.

Andrew Carnegie, the great industrialist of the late nineteenth and early twentieth centuries, was once asked the secret of his success. "Always having people around me who are smarter than I am" was his answer. What a contrast to a pastor I knew who refused to allow church members to do hospital and shut-in visitation, even though the needs were far greater than the staff could adequately handle! His insecurities that others might do it worse or might do it better than he meant those in need were not being served.

So what is the place of spiritual gifts? I want to highlight only a few points. First, spiritual gifts are given to each Christian for the good of the body of Christ (1 Cor 12:7). In Ephesians Paul says that the gifts are "to equip the saints for the work of ministry, for building up the body of Christ" (4:12). Their purpose is to prepare all Christians for the job of strengthening the church—not just the pros but us amateurs too.

Second, and as a consequence of the first, gifts are not for building ourselves up. They don't raise our status with God at all, nor does the number of gifts we possess. In the parable of the talents (Mt 25: 14-30), the master gave equal treatment to the two servants who doubled the talents given them, even though one had ten and the other four. Both were rewarded identically: "Well done, good and faithful servant; you have been faithful over little, I will set you over much; enter into the joy of your master" (Mt 25:21, 23). The gifts are simply the means God has chosen to use to do his work. They are Spirit-filled activities which glorify God, totally independent of the holiness of their possessors. This is clearly seen in the Corinthian church—one of the most problem-filled, contentious and morally lax churches Paul dealt with. Yet they seemed to exercise the gifts more than most.

Our personal spirituality is determined by the fruit of the Spirit in our lives (Gal 5:16-26) rather than the gifts of the Spirit. In 1 Corinthians 12:31—13:3 Paul calls love (the characteristic leading the list of the fruit) the "excellent way." Without love the gifts are "nothing." For the purpose of the gifts is to help others grow in the faith—certainly an act of love.

Third, as spiritual gifts are for the benefit of others and not ourselves, the benefit they bring is a spiritual one. This helps distinguish gifts from natural talents. I have heard some of the finest sacred music ever composed sung with superb technique and faultless pitch. But I was unmoved. At other times I have heard fourthrate religious music sung by a well-meaning but untalented Christian and have been near tears as God moved me to worship and confess through the song. I should also say that I have experienced the same with excellent music exquisitely performed. The point is not how poorly or how well the work was done, but whether God worked through it. The same can be true with teaching or hospitality or generosity or administration. If such work does not ultimately move others toward God, it is merely a natural talent and not a spiritual gift.

Fourth, and most importantly, spiritual gifts are meant to glorify Jesus Christ. When Paul begins his discussion of gifts in 1 Corinthians 12, he sets the context by saying, "Now concerning spiritual gifts, brethren, I do not want you to be uninformed. . . . I want you to understand that no one speaking by the Spirit of God ever says 'Jesus be cursed!' and no one can say 'Jesus is Lord' except by the Holy Spirit" (1 Cor 12:1, 3). This is the main purpose of the work of the Spirit—to direct the attention of men and women to Jesus Christ, the Lord of the universe. As our Lord himself said, "When the Spirit of Truth comes . . . he will glorify me, for he will take what is mine and declare it to you" (Jn 16:13-14).

How then do we cultivate gifts in others? Several ideas suggest themselves from what has just been said. First, by focusing attention on Christ. If we *direct people to Jesus,* doing all that we can to develop their relationship with him, their knowledge of him, their obedience to him, their worship of him—the Spirit, by definition, will be working freely in their lives as he wills, for "no one can say 'Jesus is Lord' except by the Spirit."

Second, in discipling others we should *concentrate on the fruit of the Spirit.* We are to build in Christlike character of love, joy, peace, patience, kindness, goodness, faithfulness, gentleness and self-control. This is Phyllis's and my primary goal for our children. A lofty ideal, but one which the Spirit also desires.

We need, third, to *encourage acts of service* to the whole community of believers. We should not hesitate to tell people when we see evidence of gifts in them. As with praising others, God is not glorified when we hold back our affirmation. We can also create opportunities for people to exercise the gifts they do or might suspect they have. If Jim has a gift of faith, we could create a channel for funneling prayer requests to him even though we may have never done anything like that before. If Helen has a gift of counseling, we can put her in touch with colleges that have courses in that area so her ability can be developed. We can also inform others about the gifts. Those sections of Ray Stedman's *Body Life* or Charles Hummel's *Fire in the Fireplace* that deal with gifts are quite helpful. We should remind everyone that each person has some way to contribute to the maturing of the body of Christ. "We, though many, are one body in Christ, and individually members one of another" (Rom 12:5).

Delegate: Setting Ten to Work

A facilitator is also one who delegates. When John went into the hospital for surgery, Phyllis called around to friends. To one she asked, "Will you schedule those in our Sunday-school class to get meals to John's family for the next three weeks?" To another, "Will you make sure Janet [their five-year-old daughter] has a sitter or a place to stay while Donna visits John in the hospital?" To another, "Can you organize people to go with Donna to visit John?" In each case she made sure people knew their job was not to cook all the meals or do all the sitting or give all the rides but to find others to do these. Phyllis not only delegated, she delegated the job of delegating! When she gave a job, she also gave people the freedom to decide how to do it (usually within specified limits). If we don't do that, we keep the authority for making decisions, and therefore we really haven't delegated.

Good delegators also give people the resources to do the job. When Phyllis delegated the meals for John's family, she also suggested the resources of people from the church to help. At other times a needed resource will be sufficient training or instruction in how a task is done. Money, time and equipment or tools can also be needed resources. When Jesus delegated the task of making disciples of all nations, he also gave the resource of his presence. "Lo, I am with you always, to the close of the age" (Mt 28:20).

Next, the task itself must be clear. The job was not, "Do something to help John" but "Get people to go with Donna to the hospital." Finally, the task must be accepted by the other person. Phyllis didn't say, "I hope you'll do this" and walk off. She waited until she got a definite answer one way or the other.

But what does delegating have to do with facilitating? Delegating is a way of bringing out the best in others, helping them to develop skills and confidence for larger tasks. Earlier I mentioned the parable of the talents. When the master delegated responsibility for a few talents, the servants who proved faithful were promised to be given even more responsibility. When David was a boy, he was given the job of watching sheep. He fulfilled the task of caring for and protecting the sheep by killing a lion and a bear that attacked the flock. This prepared him for the greater challenge of facing Goliath (1 Sam 17:33-35). Through these experiences the best was brought out in the two faithful servants and in David.

Delegating also encourages commitment to group goals. If I have been given the job of organizing music for our weekly group meetings, I am likely to be more concerned about the whole meeting than if I were a mere participant. I have a stake in how things go, and I'm much more inclined to cooperate in all aspects of the event and of the group. I am motivated to do my best because I feel that I am an important part of what goes on. Often we expect people to volunteer to help. They should know, after all, that there is a lot of work to do. But being asked to help, even in a small task, can make people feel that they are wanted and needed—that they belong. Thus loyalty to the group increases.

Another reason for delegating is that more can be done by two than by one. This would seem to be as obvious as lightning in the middle of the night. But the reluctance of so many people to delegate belies this. We think we can do it faster and better ourselves.

Once I was directing a writers' workshop of about twenty people. Elaine volunteered to find out the details about the recreational facilities that were available. Later she reported that we could purchase 50¢ passes each day for the health center. Then she said, "I strongly suggest that you find someone besides yourself to collect the money and hand out the passes." I was surprised at her directness, but she had quickly spotted in me a tendency to try to do everything. It was a small workshop. Certainly I could handle details like this and free the rest to do what they came for—to write. But I failed to realize that I too could do a better job if I were freed to focus on my priority (helping the others to write) instead of on details. My initial thought of doing it myself was simply shortsighted. And I also would have lost an opportunity to help someone else feel more a part of the group by asking that person to do this task.

A youth pastor at a church I know does much the same thing I tried to do. He refuses to allow any youth activities of any kind to go on when he isn't there. So if he is out of town—nothing happens. When he took part of the youth group out for a week-long back pack, nothing happened for those who were left behind even though there were people willing and able to lead. So the youth of the church suffer, the body suffers, because the youth pastor has failed to realize that two can do more than one.

Initially it can take extra time to delegate, to train, to instruct in a job. It always takes longer to show someone how to do something than to do it yourself. But failure to delegate because of this is almost always a failure to live by priorities. It keeps you bogged down in details and prevents you from taking the necessary periodic looks at the big picture. You can't ask, "Are there other needs to meet? Are there new groups to reach out to? Are there problems developing that need resolution?" Failure to delegate means imprisonment to daily maintenance functions.

There were many things I liked about Jimmy Carter as President. But one of the many criticisms he received was his inability to delegate properly. Whether or not White House staff really needed his personal approval to use the tennis court, such a story indicates his preference for trying to do it all himself instead of concentrating on what was truly important. It was a lesson he learned only slowly during his four years in Washington.

To say you can do it better yourself is to say you don't trust others —or that you trust yourself too much. None of us is indispensable. God can raise up rocks to fulfill his goals. Humbly we should remember that he has chosen to use us—all of us—to do his will. By delegating we acknowledge our finiteness and our dependence on others in the body of Christ.

If anyone didn't need anyone to help him to do a job, it was Jesus. Certainly God incarnate with armies of angels at his disposal could handle things on his own quite well, thank you. Yet he delegated. Mark's Gospel says, "He . . . called to him those whom he desired; and they came to him. And he appointed twelve, to be with him, and to be sent out to preach and have authority to cast out demons" (3:13-15). Here we find the four aspects of delegation mentioned earlier. He asked for and received acceptance of his call from the Twelve. He gave them authority to fulfill the task. He gave them the resources necessary by being with them to teach and train them. And he gave specific tasks: to preach and to cast out demons. And after a training period, he sent them out to do just this, giving them even clearer and more specific instructions (Mk 6:7-13; Lk 9:1-6). Later he sent out seventy disciples for similar work (Lk 10:1-24). And, as I said before, the Great Commission itself has been delegated to us.

Already I have mentioned a few practical basics of delegating: get a clear acceptance or rejection of the task; give clear instructions; offer all the resources needed to fulfill the task; begin by delegating minor responsibilities so that others can grow into major ones. Let me add a few more.

Begin by asking the right person. Don't ask the most capable to do a trivial chore or least capable to do a monumental one. Then when you do ask, express confidence. Tell the person why the job is important and why you feel he or she can do it.

Afterward, check back to see how progress is coming. If there is a problem, don't merely give a pep talk. Help the person. Be sure some concrete steps are agreed on before you sign off. If Jane hasn't called anyone to lead small groups at the retreat, make sure she has a list of people to call. Help her decide who she will call first, second and so on. Ask her when she plans to call. Be specific. But don't talk down to her as if she were a little lost girl. And in general, don't take the job back and do it yourself.

Last, remember the final responsibility is yours. If those to whom you delegate do fail, it is your failure more than theirs. Do not try to shift blame to them from yourself. Those you ask to help must not feel that you will cheerfully help them to the electric chair should something go wrong. They need to know you will support them while still being honest about your mistakes and theirs.

Delegation can be an unfortunate word because it conjures notions of organizational charts and harsh business practices. Yet for Christians it should mean the very thing we've been saying about facilitating all along: "To equip the saints for the work of ministry, for building up the body of Christ" (Eph 4:12). It means that the whole body builds the whole body. It means God is glorified because his fullness is shown more completely by the activity of the church than by that of any individual or individuals. Indeed, what is his plan hidden for ages? "That through the church the manifold wisdom of God might now be made known" (Eph 3:10).

Supplicate: Fighting the Battle
A facilitator appreciates, initiates, cultivates, delegates and supplicates. While the other aspects of facilitating can be used or set aside or mixed together almost at will, prayer is not an option for spiritual

leaders seeking to bring out the best in others. Prayer is not the last ingredient in a recipe. It is not the last mile of a race. Prayer is the race itself. It is not a weapon in the battle. It is the battle.

In Ephesians 6 Paul compares our spiritual warfare to earthly warfare. In verses 13-17 he urges us to put on the whole armor of God: girding ourselves with truth, having the breastplate of righteousness, covering our feet with the gospel of peace, taking the shield of faith, the helmet of salvation and the sword of the Spirit.

When soldiers have prepared themselves in this way, do they stand around and look menacing when an enemy is near? No, they fight. Thus once Paul has dressed his spiritual soldier, he immediately goes on to say, "Pray." This is the battle. A spiritual battle against principalities and powers, against spiritual hosts of wickedness in heavenly places, is fought with spiritual weapons of truth, righteousness, faith and salvation through prayer. The battle is prayer.

How seldom, though, our prayer bears the marks of cosmic conflict. John White writes, "You are writing a letter to a friend for whom you pray fairly regularly. What will you tell him? 'I do pray for you, Jack. I'm asking God to bless you and to lead you. I really pray. I pray he'll bless you richly.' What do the words mean? What does *bless* mean? Is the word an excuse on your part for not being specific? Is it too much trouble to think out a specific request? It is easier of course if Jack has pneumonia or if Jack's girlfriend has just been killed in a car accident. You can get your teeth into prayer under such circumstances. But if nothing dramatic is happening to Jack and if he's a Christian who's getting along reasonably well in his Christian walk, how are you supposed to pray?"[7]

White suggests we take a cue from the same letter of Paul to the Ephesians. In chapter 1 he prays "that the God of our Lord Jesus Christ, the Father of glory, may give you a spirit of wisdom and of revelation in the knowledge of him, having the eyes of your hearts enlightened, that you may know what is the hope to which he has called you, what are the riches of his glorious inheritance in the saints, and what is the immeasurable greatness of his power in us who believe, according to the working of his great might which he accomplished in Christ when he raised him from the dead" (1:17-20). Paul's vision is cosmic indeed! The knowledge of God. The hope of Christ. The power of the resurrection. These are supplications fit to do battle with "the spiritual hosts of wickedness in the heavenly places" (6:12).

Such prayer, however, requires hearts enlightened to God's purposes and plans far more profound than finding a ride home for Thanksgiving or a lost key or a friend to help with a project. While God is concerned with the details of our lives, they must all fit in the larger context of his overall goals for our discipleship in Christ. God is not a celestial bellhop salivating to serve at every ringing of the bell. He is our Lord with mighty plans for his subjects.

Our children are young and seem to have no mighty spiritual foes to vanquish now. Nonetheless, Phyllis and I try to pray in a larger context than dirty diapers and scraped knees and bad coughs and lost toys. We pray God will take Stephen's energy and enthusiasm for life and guide it into power to serve his Lord. We ask that he will take Susan's determination and turn it into steadfastness in the faith. We ask that he will take Philip's happiness and develop it into a burning joy in his Lord. Yes, we pray about the other things too, but there is a great richness in knowing we are praying toward God's ultimate goals for Stephen, Susan and Philip.

We crave the spiritual good of those we serve. We desire godliness and wisdom, love and truth, grace and insight for them. We are powerless to impart these gifts apart from the power of God. Information we can give. Techniques we can teach. Habits we can ingrain. It is beyond our finite abilities to place the glory of Christ in the lives of others. Only the Holy Spirit does this.

Mysteriously, God has still chosen to involve us in this process. He has ordained that we participate through prayer in moving his Holy Spirit to act in the lives of our friends, our families, our co-workers. The Almighty God of the universe, who needs no one and nothing, grants us the privilege of working with him as he leads his people.

This humbles us. It should also motivate us to involve others—all others—in this leadership process. God has done it with us. Can we do less with those we lead? As we saw in the last chapter, our authority is not our own. It belongs to another. So we involve others in prayer itself. As our Lord spent the night in Gethsemane before he died asking his disciples to watch and pray with him, we should solicit the prayer support of those we serve even as we pray for them. John 17 reveals much of the content of Christ's prayers that night concerning his disciples and his church, prayers we will look at again in chapter six.

Facilitators bring out the best. Through prayer God's best is put into others.

5
The Path
of
Teaching

*The true heart of thinking is to begin with ourselves, our
Author, and our end.*
Blaise Pascal

I suppose we should have guessed, but we decided to take him anyway. Stephen was two and a half and we thought it was time to
expose him to the main church service. We warned him what it
would be like and how he should behave. But being a two-and-a-
half-year-old who was very much alive, he played and talked and
asked questions and fidgeted and squirmed and swung his legs and
looked off into nowhere, apparently unimpressed by the worship
that surrounded him. Neither the hymns nor the readings nor the
sermon nor the prayers seemed to penetrate his energetic personality.

When it was all over, we returned home, much relieved, for our noon meal. During a pause in our dinner conversation, Stephen asked, "Did he ever meet the dog?"

We were used to such questions which arose from no immediately obvious context, so we asked, "Did *who* ever meet the dog?"

"The boy."

"*Which* boy?"

"The boy in the dark."

Suddenly we understood. He was not talking about a friend or a dog he had seen out the window. During the sermon, the preacher had told an extended story about a time when he and his son were lost in the dark during a fishing trip. At one point in their journey back to safety they had to choose between facing an unseen dog with a large bark or pushing through thick, flesh-cutting bramble. They chose the bramble and on the far side found a road back home.

Despite Stephen's fidgeting and apparent disinterest, the story stuck. Yet Stephen is not so unusual. How many of us walk away from a sermon and find that all we can remember are the illustrations or the jokes? Even the points of these stories have not penetrated our feeble gray matter. But the stories have stuck.

Teaching, for most of us, means lecturing in a classroom, preaching from a pulpit or, perhaps, giving a monolog to a small group of eager listeners in our living room. We think of passing on information in three-point outlines and trying to make mountains of content go down reluctant throats as smoothly as possible—with the greatest effect.

I do not mean to belittle lectures or lecturers. Certainly Jesus lectured. Think of the Sermon on the Mount (Mt 5—7) or his teaching in the synagogues and in the Temple. He gave instructions to the Twelve before sending them out to preach (Mt 10:5-42), and he was often called Rabbi or Teacher (Jn 11:8, 28; 13:13-14). But Jesus never lost sight of why he was teaching. He sought to change not only what people thought and did, but who they were. Lecturers who lose sight of these goals and merely seek to transfer so many bits of information from one head to another can be deadly. We begin treating our listeners as objects which receive our knowledge rather than as people God wishes to justify, sanctify and glorify.

While straight discourse can be effective and is appropriate on occasion, it is not the only way to teach. You do not have to be able to dazzle a crowd of two thousand or two hundred or twenty to be an effective teacher. This was not the only way Jesus taught. He used a mixture of methods which together helped those around him become the people God wanted them to be. Because he is the Master Teacher, I want in this chapter to highlight three neglected aspects of the way he taught—the use of story, the use of inductive thinking and the use of informal, natural settings. (You see, even I cannot escape three-point outlines!)

A Story to Tell

The story of the dog in the dark stuck with Stephen. What makes stories stick so much easier than principles or statistics? First, stories often deal with what is already known. Jesus sprinkled familiar objects and events throughout his parables and images. We find houses and floods, harvests and laborers, doctors and the sick, brides and bridegrooms, patches and garments, wine and wineskins, sparrows and hairs, dances and dirges, loads and yokes, sand and soil. There are hidden treasures, lost coins, stormy skies, stumbling blocks, impenitent slaves, wedding feasts and whited sepulchers. By beginning with something that we have already learned, a teacher can easily move to what we do not know yet.

Second, stories stick not only because they use familiar objects and events but also because they evoke familiar feelings. We understand what is being taught better when we feel what is being taught.

After King David took Bethsheba and had her husband killed so he could marry her, Nathan told David a story. A traveler came to a rich man, and, as was the custom, the rich man prepared a fine meal for him. But he didn't use one of his many sheep or cattle. Instead he took the ewe lamb of a poor man for the traveler's meal. Before Nathan even had the chance to draw David to compare the story to his own sin, David burst out in anger, "The man who has done this deserves to die." Nathan responded, "You are the man." The story compelled David to see the injustice he was previously able to ignore. As Nathan sharpened the story's point, David's guilt overwhelmed him. He confessed, "I have sinned against the LORD." The walls of presumptuous authority and power and right crumbled before the simple story of a poor man's sheep (2 Sam 12:1-15).

A thousand years later another prophet had a confrontation with Jewish authority. Toward the end of Jesus' ministry he encountered the Pharisees in the Temple. What had been tense before the day began grew electric when Jesus bested them in a confrontation over his authority (Mt 21:23-27).

Yet even after the antagonism had increased he proceeded to make the situation worse by comparing the Pharisees to a son who said he would obey his father but never did. He concludes, "Truly, I say to you, the tax collectors and the harlots go into the kingdom of God before you" (Mt 21:28-31).

Incredibly, Jesus did not stop even here. The Pharisees already hated him, and twice he had shown them up. Yet he insisted on telling one more story—this time about the owner of a vineyard who leased his land to tenants. At harvest time the owner sent two sets of servants to get the fruit. All the servants were killed by the tenants. Then the owner sent his son, whom he thought would be respected. The tenants killed him too. "When the owner of the vineyard comes," Jesus asked, "what will he do to those tenants?"

Although the Pharisees were piqued with Jesus, they were captured by his story. They were incensed by the wickedness of the tenants. Their answer was not simply, "He will have them executed." No, they replied, "He will put those *wretches* to a *miserable* death." The story evoked strong feelings, strong enough to overcome their anger toward Jesus, strong enough to allow Jesus for a third time to make his point to what would otherwise be unlistening Pharisees.

"Jesus said to them, 'Have you never read in the scriptures: "The very stone which the builders rejected has become the head of the corner." ... Therefore I tell you, the kingdom of God will be taken away from you and given to a nation producing the fruits of it.' When the chief priests and the Pharisees heard his parables, they perceived that he was speaking about them" (Mt 21:33-45). Through this parable, despite the threefold antagonism of the Pharisees toward Jesus, *they perceived,* they saw, they understood, they learned. Jesus taught.

We must be careful not to manipulate people with stories that bring out emotion. But we should not hesitate to use stories to overcome resistance as well as to clarify the truth we have to tell.

Stories also stick because they are human. How many of us can recall even one high-school textbook which so gripped us that to this day we are different people? Most of us trudged through them like a World War 1 soldier through a rain-filled trench. No one remembers a biology text or what was in it. Even a book about the human body is inhuman, and we forget it.

Far more likely, we remember our biology teacher who instilled a love for creation and a fascination with the mystery of life. Indeed, biology became alive through that teacher. It became human.

I remember lining up in front of Chicago's Field Museum early one morning to see what millions of others also lined up to see —the treasures of King Tutankhamen. The gold and beauty were dazzling on their own. The exhibitors, however, were wise enough to do more than display an ancient chain here and a death mask there. Through the exhibition they also told the events that led up to the 1922 discovery of the tomb by Howard Carter. More than an academic exercise, the display became a drama of human determination and success—as well as of royal power and glory.

The human quality of stories is closely linked to feelings. But, of course, we are more than a source of feelings. We are creative; we have dignity and value; we have minds. When stories touch these deep aspects of human existence, we remember them.

Stories also stick when they involve relationships. This too involves feelings because most of our feelings arise from our relationships with others. I emphasize this because so often we grow and change in relation to others.

Consider yourself. What are the key factors in who you are today? They may include events (a war, an accident, a choice of schools) or facts of life (you were raised poor, you were an only child, your mother worked). But alongside and often dominating these factors are the people who influenced you during these times.

I can point to at least four people who have helped me become who I am: my parents, who showed me the value of hard, careful work and love in the home; George, who opened to me a new relationship to God and his Word; and my wife, who has helped me see the priority of people. Many characteristics I wish I didn't have can also be traced to a few individuals. I wish I were less a perfectionist, less an intellectualizer, less a snob. I must take responsibility for these faults and not blame them on others. Yet the influence of others is there.

Relationships, people, have a profound impact on who we are. Stories then can strike deeply when they speak of this basic building block of our being. If our goal is to affect who others are, we will tell them stories, as Jesus did.

Lastly, Jesus did not just *tell* stories. Jesus is a story. He is the message. He is the Living Word. He is good news of salvation, a story about what has happened, what is happening and what will happen. We do not have a list of how-tos to give or a series of abstract principles to teach. We have a life-changing story to tell.

Learning to Think

A second neglected aspect of Jesus' teaching is that of *inductive thinking*. This means, simply, drawing your own conclusions based on your own examination of the evidence.

Three-year-old Sarah insists on trying to eat the soap in the bathtub. No amount of screaming or spanking seems to alter her peculiar taste. But once Sarah is allowed to get sick on her fill of bath bars, no screaming or spanking is needed. Based on her own examination of the evidence, Sarah concludes that she should not eat soap. This is a lesson that will stick with her a long time.

Adolescent rebellion has the same effect. What we learn about life in our high-school and college years often sticks far more than all the rules and regulations our parents might lay down. "Don't drive too fast" slows down few first-year drivers. But an accident can instantaneously transform one into a model of caution. Students away at college also seem to have amnesia about warnings not to stay up too late. But when they sleep through the test they pulled an all-nighter to study for, they don't have to remember. They figure it out themselves.

This is the first characteristic of inductive thinking: We tend to remember longer what we learn inductively because we discover the truth ourselves. It is said that we retain 10% of what we hear but 90% of what we say. I believe we also retain about 90% of what we think through for ourselves.

And if we do forget, another advantage of inductive thinking is that it is reproducible. We can retrace our steps, look at the facts again in an unbiased manner, and once more teach ourselves a lesson we will likely not forget.

God taught Adam inductively in the garden. He had already concluded that it was not good that man should be alone (Gen 2:18). But Adam had not discovered this for himself. He was at ease with God and nature. What could be more comfortable?

The Lord could have said, "Adam, you need a helper, and here she is," only to be met with the objection, "Wait a minute, Lord. I need no such thing. I'm fine. Nothing's gone wrong in the garden. What do I need a helper for? She'll just get in the way." That would have been a natural response. And even if Adam would not have objected, he might have been complacent or uninterested. In any case, God chose not to confront Adam with the solution but to allow him first to see the problem for himself.

God began not by making Eve but by first forming every kind of bird and beast. He paraded them before Adam, who proceeded to give each one a name. Having seen and named all the animals, Adam knew he was unique. There was no one else like him. He was alone (Gen 2:19-20).

The same three steps are repeated in the next verses. First, God formed the woman, then he brought her to Adam, and finally Adam named her (Gen 2:21-23). But his reaction was strikingly different. "This is bone of my bones and flesh of my flesh." In effect, he said, "Here at last is someone like me. I've seen all the birds and beasts, and I know none of them is like me. But you are, Eve. Now I have a companion to be with me." Because Adam was presented with the facts and then allowed to draw his own conclusions, Adam was ready to make the deep and lasting commitment required in marriage.

The same is true for most of us. We are more likely to hold fast to convictions we have arrived at ourselves than to ones handed to or forced upon us. Although we may share the beliefs of our parents, we usually do not come to hold these beliefs firmly until we prove them for ourselves.

Jesus used the same approach when he taught. We remember the questions asked of him by the lawyer—"Which is the great commandment in the law?" (Mt 22:36); and by the rich young man—"What must I do to inherit eternal life?" (Mk 10:17); and by Nicodemus—"How can a man be born when he is old?" (Jn 3:4). But we sometimes forget the many questions he asked others.

In the middle of a discourse he would ask questions to stimulate his listeners' thinking—"If salt has lost its taste, how shall its saltness be restored?" (Mt 5:13). Sometimes an entire exchange with the disciples was a series of questions (Mt 16:9-12). Or he would begin an encounter with questions—"What do you think, Simon? From whom do kings of the earth take toll or tribute? From their sons or from others?" (Mt 17:25).

Remarkably, however, Jesus often responded to questions put to him with still more questions (Mt 9:14-15; 12:10-11; 15:1-3; 21:23-25). When the lawyer asked Jesus "Who is my neighbor?" Jesus told the story of the good Samaritan and then asked the lawyer, "Which of these three, do you think, proved neighbor to the man who fell among the robbers?" (Lk 10:25-37).

Likewise, when the rich young man asked Jesus "Good Teacher, what must I do to inherit eternal life?" Jesus answered, "Why do you call me good? No one is good but God alone" (Mk 10:17-18). Jesus quickly drops in this question and comment and never goes back to it. He leaves it to the rich young man (and those nearby) to resolve it. Was Jesus good or not? Was God good or not? Was the man good? Could he be good enough to attain eternal life? All these questions and more whirl around this brief encounter. Jesus was content to leave many of them without explicit answers. Teaching by questions or by allowing others to observe evidence and draw conclusions can be a slow and agonizing process. While many of Jesus' questions were quite leading or rhetorical, there was one issue he allowed to remain ambiguous—his identity. He even refused to give a direct answer to his cousin John the Baptist.

John was in prison and was perhaps beginning to have doubts about this man he baptized in the Jordan. "John, calling to him two of his disciples, sent them to the Lord, saying, 'Are you he who is to come, or shall we look for another?' And when the men had come to him, they said, 'John the Baptist has sent us to you, saying, "Are you he who is to come, or shall we look for another?" ' In that hour he cured many of diseases and plagues and evil spirits, and on many that were blind he bestowed sight. And he answered them, 'Go and tell John what you have seen and heard: the blind receive their sight, the lame walk, lepers are cleansed, and the deaf hear, the dead are raised up, the poor have good news preached to them' " (Lk 7:19-22). Jesus offered John the evidence. He would recognize these activities and Jesus' summary of them from the prophet Isaiah (29:18-19; 35:5-6; 61:1). But Jesus refused to draw the final conclusion. That John must do.

Even with his disciples Jesus was slow to openly acknowledge who he was. Early in his public ministry he allowed them to see him heal the sick and cast out demons and teach with a unique and powerful authority. But they were still afraid when crossing the Sea of Galilee in a storm with him. After calming it "He said to them, 'Why are you afraid? Have you no faith?' And they were filled with awe, and said to one another, 'Who then is this, that even wind and sea obey him?' " (Mk 4:40-41).

Jesus then gave them more evidence. He raised a dead girl and fed the five thousand. Yet when he walked to them on the water one night, they were terrified, "and they were utterly astounded, for they did not understand about the loaves, but their hearts were hardened" (Mk 6:51-52).

Still, Jesus was patient. Yet eventually he asked them, "Who do men say that I am?" After they recited several possibilities, Jesus asked directly, "But who do you say that I am?" Peter answered, "You are the Christ" (Mk 8:27-29). Only then did Jesus speak openly of his Messiahship to his disciples. He may have been concerned what the Jewish authorities would do if he proclaimed his identity too soon, but I believe that he was not just being secretive. He was training committed disciples.

Jesus' slow, deliberate method contrasts to our desire for quick decisions and instant growth. Once Phyllis and I became frustrated with Bill, who was not giving Sherry, his wife, the priority she deserved over his career. Why couldn't he see what he was doing? Did he have to work late every night and Saturday too? Didn't he know what Ephesians 5 said? Christ died for the church. It seemed he couldn't sacrifice an hour to devote solely to her. We had to remind ourselves he had only been a Christian a couple of years. God would change Bill, but not on our timetable. He wanted to develop slow, sure growth in him in this area. Our impatience might only drive Bill away. Our role was to continue to expose Bill to the Bible's teaching on marriage, to model such a marriage before him and to pray that God would change him.

Often we hear the phrase "Only take people as far as they are ready to go." This is another way of stating the principle of teaching by inductive thinking. We must allow people to grow at their own pace. Each person is an individual. God has a special plan for how that person will grow as well as for who he or she will become. We cannot teach assuming everyone will develop at the same pace or end up at the same destination. When people are ready to learn, they will, through God's power, our prayer and our availability to them.

Phyllis and I believe one of the most valuable traits we can instill in our children is the ability to make decisions. We begin by limiting their choices to two, making sure both options are acceptable. Then we affirm the choice the child makes.

"Susan, would you like hot cereal or cold cereal for breakfast?"

"Hot cereal."

"That's a good decision you made, Susan. It's cold this morning, isn't it?"

This approach avoids the natural human distaste for imposed solutions.

"Susan, we are going to have hot cereal this morning; it's cold out."

"But I don't want hot cereal. I want cold cereal."

"It's hot cereal or nothing."

We avoid tears and a fight by letting Susan decide. But something more important also happens. We help Susan grow in her ability to make more difficult decisions, to learn to live with the consequences of those decisions, and to grow in her confidence to make decisions. Then, when the choices become more difficult (like deciding whether to take drugs or lose friends) and we are not around to help, she will, we hope, have learned how to decide such things for herself.

We call people to "make a decision for Christ," yet too often we believe that is the last decision they have to make as Christians. Our Christian lives are full of decisions and crossroads. How will I confront Mary about her incessant sarcasm? What will I do to help Jim while his dad is in the hospital? How much time should I spend studying, how much at church and how much with family this semester? If we try to spoon-feed those in our care, they will never get the practice of dealing with such problems themselves. They will remain immature.

Once every week Phyllis and I open up the Scripture with about thirty friends to try to find God's wisdom on everyday questions just such as these. We read a passage and ask questions. We try to help the group figure out answers for themselves. Sometimes the answers are right, as we see it, and sometimes not. But we try never to condemn or criticize any contribution. We offer our observations, but few will believe what we say just because we say it. They have to see things for themselves. In this way they have direct, undiluted contact with God's Word. No human mediator is needed. Because their involvement is direct, because they are required to think through the passage themselves, they retain what they learn.

The results have been slow but sure. People who would rarely open the Bible on their own now do so regularly. Their awareness of God in their lives has been heightened. A year of lecturing, I believe, would have accomplished little of this. But, like the people of the Samaritan village, their belief in Jesus has been far stronger after a direct encounter with him than after a mere report from someone else (Jn 4:39-42).

You have heard the saying "Give me a fish; I eat for a day. Teach me to fish; I eat for a lifetime." Telling the truth is good. But what if we are gone tomorrow. Where will our hearers find the truth then? Who will tell them the difference between what is right and what is wrong? It is better to teach people to find the truth for themselves. Although it is harder to learn to fish than to take a fish, the results of the first far outlast those of the second.

Let us allow, let us encourage people to have direct contact with God and his Word. Let us not be mediators of truth and wisdom, offering only a diet of predigested platitudes. Let others wrestle with God as Jacob did and question God as Abraham did. Let us remember that our calling as teachers is not just to pass on data but to help people grow in Christ. Learning to think for themselves is part of that maturity.

Learning in Life

A third aspect of Jesus' method of teaching that I want to highlight is the use of informal, natural settings. He did not rely, as we have seen, solely on the formal lecture hall or pulpit. He took advantage of every casual encounter to affect people's lives.

Jesus visited the home of Simon the Pharisee for dinner. A prostitute came in during the meal and began anointing Jesus' feet. Simon wondered to himself whether Jesus really knew who the woman was. Certainly a true prophet would know and wouldn't allow such a woman to carry on that way. So Jesus used this informal setting to teach Simon through a story about two men whose respective debts of five hundred and fifty denarii were canceled. At the end Jesus asked, "Which of them will love [the creditor] more?" (Lk 7:36-50).

The lessons for Simon were many in this seemingly simple episode. First, of course, was the proverb Jesus drew out of the story and the question—"Her sins, which are many, are forgiven, for she loved much; but he who is forgiven little, loves little." Next were the questions Simon surely asked himself: Have I been forgiven much or little? Do I love God much or little? Third, Simon likely wondered what kind of host he had been. Jesus had said, "I entered your house, you gave me no water for my feet, but she has wet my feet with her tears and wiped them with her hair. You gave me no kiss, but from the time I came in she has not ceased to kiss my feet. You did not anoint my head with oil, but she has anointed my feet with ointment." He probably wondered, Was I inconsiderate? Was I so caught up in my own importance that I forgot my guest? Lastly, Simon was taught about Jesus' identity. At the beginning Simon had asked himself if Jesus were a prophet. At the end, "those who were at table with him began to say among themselves, 'Who is this, who even forgives sins?' "

As a result of Jesus' teaching in this informal setting, Simon was left with more questions than answers. And Jesus was quite content to leave Simon in this mental disarray. He had broken Simon's preconceptions about sin and forgiveness and holiness—and about Jesus. He left Simon to sort through repercussions of this teaching event that Simon (and the others at the meal) might never have faced in the Temple.

We too should not ignore the opportunities that everyday occurrences provide for teaching. We need not find a moral behind every test or in every tuna-noodle casserole. But we can use life to learn.

We find similar examples when Jesus calmed the sea for the panic-filled disciples or when he healed on the sabbath or when he told the disciples not to keep the children away from him.

Such learning opportunities will not be ours to share with those we teach unless we are with them in casual, everyday settings. A trip to the bank, a response to having your car repaired, a birthday party are all places to learn. This leads us to the topic of the next chapter, which takes up another way of influencing others—being a role model.

Who Is the Teacher?

Before leaving the topic of teaching, however, I want to consider what kind of persons teachers should be. For teaching, as I have said, is not necessarily the act of imparting knowledge. It is changing lives. Who we are will profoundly affect the way others learn from us.

First, a good teacher has humility. How often I have listened to a sermon or a talk only to think to myself, "I could do that. No, I could do it better." Such an attitude does not lend itself to learning. No one likes know-it-alls. We turn off people who come across with all the answers faster than a flap of a fly's wings. No one would like, much less learn from, an arrogant Andy Le Peau at the podium.

I have agonized over the writing of this book. What do I have to offer others about being a leader? Better that I ask this question than, Why hasn't someone asked me to write a book on leadership? We should not be quick to want to teach. James says, "Let not many of you become teachers, my brethren, for you know that we who teach shall be judged with greater strictness" (3:1). We will be judged by the very teachings we give others. We should therefore be cautious about the number of absolutes we dispense. Even though we possess absolute truth, we do not possess absolute wisdom. May God grant us more.

Next, a good teacher is patient. We should be willing to wait, to allow people to grow at their own pace. We often forget it took us five, ten or fifteen years to learn a particular lesson about the Christian life. We should be willing to let others take time as well.

Related to this is the last point. We should learn to be at peace with unresolved questions—in our lives and in the lives of those we teach. The ultimate end of even unresolved questions is growth.

Many times people wondered who Jesus was, and many times he did not answer. Often it is better to raise curiosity and leave people in tension than to resolve issues before the right time. Their search, if it is sincere, will increase in intensity. If not, or if they are otherwise not ready to hear, no amount of information will help.

It is easy enough to *say* it is better to let these questions remain unresolved. Often it is hard to do. Tonight I watched the news report about a child who was bludgeoned to death by his parents. Questions race through me. Why? Why? How evil we are! Why do you let such things happen, God? Maybe the world would be better off after a nuclear war—the Lord knows we deserve it. Why? Why a child?

As these unanswered questions grind away in my stomach, perhaps God is helping me to grow in faith and trust in him, in love and concern for a hurting world. Perhaps a quick answer from God would not work such maturing in me. It is easy to say. It is not easy to live. Yet I believe. God is teaching me.

6
The Path
of
Modeling

*To be a leader a man must have followers. And to have
followers, a man must have their confidence. Hence the supreme
quality for a leader is unquestionably integrity.
. . . If a man's associates find him guilty of phoniness, if
they find that he lacks forthright integrity, he will fail.
His teachings and actions must square with each other. The
first great need, therefore, is integrity and high purpose.*
Dwight Eisenhower

At a state college in Iowa, a group of Christian students were having
problems. Most felt excluded from and unwanted by the leadership
committee of the group. Communication was poor, while apathy,
on the one hand, and frustration, on the other, developed among
them.

This problem continued to grow during the fall term. But suddenly, after the winter break, the ill feelings dissolved. The group
no longer felt excluded from the leadership team. A new mood of
unity and enthusiasm began to permeate. What had happened?

Unknown to the group at large, tension between two of the leaders, Martin and Dave, had been growing that fall. They had been keeping their distance from each other as much as possible. Despite none of the other students knowing this feud existed and the feud being solely between the two leaders, the whole group was affected. When Martin and Dave were finally able to heal their rift in December (again without anyone else knowing), the effects were again soon felt by the rest of the Christian students. They then sensed a oneness with the leadership and the group as a whole.

Who we are as leaders can often be as important or more important than how we lead. Whether we like it or not, we are being watched. And not just watched—our example is being followed. Leaders cannot choose to model or not to model for others. Because they are leaders, they model.

This seems so obvious it almost seems foolish to say it. Yet many of us forget the massive implications our lives have on those we lead. I know someone as sensitive to criticism as a snowflake to the breeze. His movement seems to be affected by every subtle shift of the wind. The result? Those he supervises have become snowflakes too. They gauge their actions and comments as much by the criticism they are likely to receive as by Scripture. For they know that any chill breeze that blows his way will soon blow their way too—only this time it will be a little warmer.

Likewise, sociologists know that one of the groups of parents most likely to be child abusers are those who themselves were abused as children—often despite their conscious determination to act otherwise. Similarly, but positively, children whose parents never divorced are themselves less likely to divorce.

A Relief and a Burden
Who we are as leaders is thus a vital issue. The model we present will not guarantee that those we serve will act the same as we do—be it good or ill. Even one who followed Christ and observed his ex-

ample for three years betrayed him in the end. Each person is an individual responsible to God for his or her life.

Instead of being a way to force others to change, the model we offer should be a statement of who we are and of who we desire others to be. We should not seek to have others live just the way we do (pray daily at 6 A.M.; read Lewis, Merton and *Doonesbury;* evangelize football players), but to be the kind of people we are (faithful, loving, honest, open, truthful, peaceful, joyful). This calling is at once a relief and a burden.

It is a relief to know that it is not necessary to perfect a particular package of techniques—especially if we find ourselves ill-suited for certain practices. Bruce always struck me as the perfect evangelist —a role in which I was uncomfortable. He could befriend anyone anywhere and have Christianity in the air between them as naturally as a leaf falling on an autumn day. I admired Bruce greatly but was simultaneously stung by my own sense of inadequacy. He seemed to have perfected the one right approach. I was stunned one day to hear him say, "The most important thing to remember about evangelism is that you do it the way it fits you best as an individual. Don't try to imitate me or anyone else. Do what is natural for the way God made you." What a refreshing word that was! Even Bruce, who seemed so self-assured, was merely confident in who he was and how to evangelize in light of his God-given personality. I did not have to use his techniques. But I was certainly motivated by his commitment to spread God's Word.

Our calling to be who we desire others to be can also be a burden. Developing character to pass on to others is more serious as well as more difficult than developing techniques to pass on. It is more serious because the impact lasts longer.

Today we remember Polycarp, one of the early church leaders, as a man of gentleness. As a young man, he had apparently learned much from the elderly John, the apostle of love. This characteristic lasted throughout his life. A technique will not tend to stay with a person. It will be forgotten, changed or left in disuse.

A character trait will also be found (or sorely missed) in a variety of situations. Gentleness, for example, is called for while encouraging, rebuking, teaching, planning, evangelizing, helping, caring, directing and serving. A technique for helping can only be exercised in that one setting.

Hard to Be Human

Being an irrepressible middle-of-the-roader, I must say that I do not mean that techniques are bad and completely to be avoided. I use methods and routines all the time. I have a planning outline I am very fond of and believe to be quite helpful to people in a wide range of circumstances. Such techniques can save a lot of time and hard work. (I don't have to reread the New Testament every time I want to explain the gospel. I can remember the basic points.)

Character, however, must always come before technique and must always rule over it. I should not blurt out the same verses in the same order when I witness. Rather a Christlike character tempers my technique. I look first at the person in front of me and discern his or her needs, wants and uniqueness. Then I know which aspects of God's truth and love are most appropriate for this person. In other words, character makes the technique human.

The irony is that we have more difficulty being human than we do being mechanical. The Pharisees mechanically applied the law of the sabbath in an attempt to prevent Jesus from performing a compassionate and human act of healing (Mk 3:1-6). Jesus told his disciples not to use the technique the pagans use for prayer (repeating phrases over and over) but instead to pray following the example he gave them in what we call the Lord's Prayer (Mt 6:7-15). The irony grows because we have turned this very example of prayer into a technique. We repeat it over and over mindlessly, believing that this is the way to communicate with God.

Mindlessness also afflicts informal prayer. A friend once told me he learned a valuable lesson from a Roman Catholic about "heaping up empty phrases" in vain repetition. "Extemporaneous prayer," he said, "can be as vainly repetitious as liturgical prayer. At how many prayer meetings have you heard the evangelical formula, "We just really want to thank you, Lord . . . "? Even the casual becomes formalized.

Our society has created technology and techniques and then bowed down to them. The church has all too willingly followed the world's lead in seeking the best methods to develop better programs, bigger buildings and bulgier budgets. Again, methods need not be automatically rejected as evil. But I don't need to encourage more techniques. There are already plenty. What we all need is to develop godly character. Of this there is precious little.

Look at the list of qualifications Paul laid out for a bishop. "Now a bishop must be above reproach, the husband of one wife, temperate, sensible, dignified, hospitable, an apt teacher, no drunkard, not violent but gentle, not quarrelsome, and no lover of money. He must manage his own household well, keeping his children submissive and respectful in every way; for if a man does not know how to manage his own household, how can he care for God's church? He must not be a recent convert, or he may be puffed up with conceit and fall into the condemnation of the devil; moreover he must be well thought of by outsiders, or he may fall into reproach and the snare of the devil" (1 Tim 3:2-7). We find little on fund raising or money management. Instead, a bishop is to be "no lover of money." We find little on effective use of time. Instead a bishop is to be "sensible." We find little on style of leadership. Instead, he should be "gentle, not quarrelsome." Similar qualifications are called for in the next paragraph for deacons (1 Tim 3:8-13).

One proven ability that is mentioned is the capacity to "manage his own household." This does not necessarily imply that a Christian leader must be married. Rather, it highlights a principle similar to that found in the parable of the talents. In that story the master responds to each of the two servants who doubled their master's money by saying, "Well done, good and faithful servant, you have been faithful over a little, I will set you over much; enter into the joy of your master" (Mt 25:21, 23). Those who have proven reliable in one task can be trusted with larger ones. Those with peaceful households show that they qualify for a role in caring for a larger group of God's people. Those who are apt teachers in a small group show a basic qualification for teaching in wider circles.

Look again at the kind of household Paul calls for. One with children who memorize Scripture regularly and who sing in the choir and who help in community projects? No. Children who are "submissive and respectful." Children who show godly character traits, not those who show expertise in methods. Where do they learn these traits? From parents with godly character.

Materialistic Spirituality

What do we most want to accomplish with our modeling? What do we most want people to learn? Do we want people to learn to have daily quiet times at 6 A.M. or to yearn for God's company? Do we want people to learn how to organize food co-ops or to act out of compassion for the poor? Wanting the first type of learning betrays a materialistic view of spirituality; it betrays a failure to comprehend the cross.

When we evangelize, we tell people that Christ has done it all, died once to save the ungodly, and that there is nothing we can do to make ourselves acceptable to God that Christ has not already done on Calvary. Yet as soon as that person steps over the line and relinquishes the right to control his life and acknowledges God's reign in his heart, our message changes. We revert to a mechanical—yes, works-oriented—perspective on what brings one close to God. To the new convert we say, "Tithe. Pray. Give. Care. Work. Then you will be in the Almighty's palm." How mechanistic! Such acts in and of themselves are useless. We might as well suggest that they sacrifice six chickens each weekend and burn incense.

Christ's cross covers us after conversion as well as before. Christ's cross has won not only our redemption but also our sanctification and our glorification. Our holiness lies not in ourselves but in him who sits at the right hand of the Father. "You shall be holy; for I the LORD your God am holy" (Lev 19:2). Yet on our own we are just as incapable of being holy now as before becoming Christians. Whatever holiness we have is not earned. It is what God chooses to give us through his Son.

How do we attain this holiness then? "As therefore you received Christ Jesus the Lord, so live in him" (Col 2:6). How did we attain new life in the first place? Through faith. How do we sustain our new life? Through faith. "So live in him," Paul says, "rooted and built up in him and established in the faith, just as you were taught" (Col 2:6-7).

In another letter Paul told the Ephesians, "By grace you have been saved through faith; and this is not your own doing, it is the gift of God" (Eph 2:8), confirming for us that the way of salvation is all of God's doing. But often we fail to read on. "For we are his workmanship, created in Christ Jesus for good works, which God prepared beforehand, that we should walk in them" (Eph 2:10). Not only is our salvation from God, so are our good works. Our being and doing in Christ are God's doing. He made us in Christ, and he prepared beforehand the good we are to do. By grace through faith we are born anew. By grace through faith we continue to live in him anew. And this is not our own doing; it is the gift of God.

What has all this to do with modeling, much less leading? A great deal. We must have a firm grasp on the baton of God's priorities if we ever expect to pass it on to others. Yet we simply do not believe that who we are is more important than what we do. We do not believe that who we are comes from Christ. We do not believe.

I do not believe. Recently I led a Bible study that made the Edsel look like a superstar. (You don't know what the Edsel was? That just shows how successful the study was.) People didn't understand my questions. When I explained what I meant, they ignored what I had to say and went their own way. When they did understand, they disagreed with my emphasis. A flop. A disaster. A bomb.

A week later I talked with Pat, a new member of the study who had been having some significant personal problems. I asked how she was enjoying the group. "Oh, it's great. It's the best thing that has happened in my Christian life. Especially last week! People had so many questions and struggles and doubts. And that's just where I am. It's so encouraging to know there are others wrestling in the same way I am."

My strikeout was God's home run. I thought that if I had just improved my questioning technique or had spent more time preparing, then the study would have been a success. I had tried to accept people with all their doubts and dilemmas and even with their disdain for God. But I did not believe that that was more important than "being a good Bible study leader." I did not believe that the concern and openness I displayed would have greater impact than how much I knew about the Bible. I was wrong.

Watched on Purpose
Earlier I said that people watch us and become like us whether we like it or not. If we do in fact want people to be like us, one of the first things we can do is to let them watch us on purpose. That is, after all, the essence of modeling.

Yet those in official positions of leadership are not the only ones who can or should model. Henry has the fruit of kindness paired nicely with his gift of hospitality. What could be better than to pair Henry with someone who wants to grow in this way? Maria has developed the fruit of self-control over her once harsh temper. Perhaps someone struggling with overeating could learn from and be encouraged by her.

We should be getting people together to have just this kind of influence on one another because none of us is strong in all areas of Christian character. While we may be able to give sound advice on a problem, people may only believe our answers are true if they see someone living it out. This may require a model we cannot offer. Thus the whole body of Christ is involved in modeling, not just designated leaders.

Modeling also need not be formal. One can learn much about being a Christian by doing common activities with a more mature Christian. As I mentioned in the last chapter, going to the bank, watching a ball game, helping a friend fix a car, visiting a sick relative in the hospital—all are situations in which we can grow by seeing godly character lived out.

Jesus invited the disciples originally just to follow him. They were not expected initially to do much ministry. They were just to watch and listen. They traveled with him from place to place (Lk 8:1) and watched him interact with the Pharisees, with the sick, with the possessed, with the crowds. They saw him pray and teach and calm storms. Then he sent them out to work and help others (Lk 9:1-6).

Like Father, Like Son
Remarkably, the model Jesus offered his disciples was a model he himself had seen in another. The Son followed the examples of his Father. This theme permeates John's Gospel. One of the first hints is in 3:31-32. "He [Jesus] who comes from above is above all. He

bears witness to what he has seen and heard." When Jesus came to earth, he proclaimed what he had seen in heaven. What do we learn from this heavenly eyewitness? "That God is true" (v. 33).

What the Father has handed over to the Son becomes clearer in chapter 5. Indeed, not only did Jesus receive his message from the Father, but "the Son can do nothing of his own accord, but only what he sees the Father doing; for whatever he does, that the Son does likewise" (v. 19). In particular, the Son gives life to the dead as the Father does (v. 21), judges as he hears the Father judge (v. 30) and teaches as the Father taught him (8:28; 15:15). Just as the Father sent his Son into the world, so the Son sent others into the world (13:20; 17:18). Finally, "as the Father has loved me, so have I loved you" (15:9). This runs directly contrary to our normal patterns of thinking. How many boyfriends or girlfriends have you told, "To the degree that you've loved me, I've loved someone else"? Of course we don't say that. Rather it's "as much as you love me, I love you still more"—or some such sentiment. We expect to return love to its source. We love people who love us. But the pattern the Father and Son have set for us is to pass on love to others, not just to pass it back.

How uncomfortable we are with such thinking! If Jim helps me with my math homework, I've got to help him with his French. If Ruth loans me her car when mine is in the shop, I have to do the same. If I can't return the favor, I'm ill at ease. I'm in debt.

After Phyllis and I first moved into our house, we spent considerable time remodeling. Dave, our next-door neighbor, was doing the same, only he was three years ahead of us. So I often found myself over at Dave's, borrowing tools and getting advice on how to put in the vent for the dryer or get my ceiling tiles square. I certainly appreciated his help, but I could seldom return it since he was too far ahead of me in knowledge and experience.

Once I mentioned that I felt bad because he'd done so much for us and we had so little to offer him in return. "Oh, don't worry about it," he said. "I learned what I know from Russ across the street. And I haven't been able to help him much. So I pass it on to you. And you'll help someone else." And of course he was right. I have. But it was so freeing to know I was not obligated to pass it back to him. Rather, I was to share it freely with others.

As I Have Loved You
Sharing fix-it know-how is a weak illustration for explaining such a monumental truth. Divine love was modeled by the Father toward the Son, who offers the same model to us, which we are likewise to offer to others. Before his death, Jesus made explicit what he had been trying to teach his disciples by example all along, "Love one another as I have loved you" (Jn 15:12). His command was that we follow his example.

Christ showed his love for his disciples in a number of ways. First, *by praying for them.* Before he chose his twelve closest followers, he prayed all night (Lk 6:12-13). Since the Bible is silent at this point, we can only guess the substance of his prayer: that the Father would be with him in his choosing; that those he picked would learn and grow in godliness; that they would remain steadfast after his death in proclaiming the coming kingdom.

On another occasion an argument arose among the disciples as to who was greatest. Apparently they had not learned fully how to love one another. Yet Jesus took this opportunity to teach them just this lesson. He began by pointing out that although he was greater than any of them, he served (Lk 22:24-27). The implication is clear. They were to serve too.

Jesus immediately went on to give an example of his loving service to them. He turned to Simon Peter, who was no doubt in the middle of the argument, and said, "Simon, Simon, behold, Satan demanded to have you, that he might sift you like wheat, but I have prayed for you that your faith may not fail; and when you have turned again, strengthen your brethren" (Lk 22:31-32). He showed his love for Simon by praying that he would withstand temptation. Jesus also prayed that his disciples would receive the Spirit of truth (Jn 14:16-17). This Spirit would comfort them in their grief, give them peace in the midst of trouble and empower them in ministry.

John 17 provides the fullest instance of how Jesus showed his love to the disciples in prayer (vv. 6-19). He asks that the Father would keep them in his name, guarding them, protecting them from the evil one. He asks that his joy fill them as well. He asks that they be sanctified in truth, made holy, set apart for God's purpose of spreading the good news.

We too show our love for one another, for those we lead, by praying. Jesus' prayers were not of the caliber of helping people to pass tests or of getting enough money to go on vacation—though God is concerned about every aspect of our lives. Rather, his prayers for his disciples focused on more lasting matters—matters of character, matters of God's ultimate purposes, matters of the battle with Satan. Our prayers, out of our love for others, should likewise center on matters of greatest importance.

A second way Jesus showed his love for his disciples was *by listening to them.* These people must have been frustratingly dense. They watched him heal and cast out demons, but in a boat in a storm he had to calm the waves and ask, "Why are you afraid? Have you no faith?" (Mk 4:40). Later their unbelief is still unchecked when they are confronted helplessly with several thousand hungry people—not once but twice (Mk 6:35-37 and 8:1-4).

The Gospels are full of such incidents. While Jesus' heart undoubtedly burned that they would understand and believe, his intensity never overflowed to insensitivity. He patiently continued to answer their questions and repeat explanations and illustrations.

(For example, see Mt 13:36-43 and Jn 14:6-11.)

Phyllis receives a string of phone calls each day from a wide variety of people with an even wider variety of topics to discuss. Our doorsill is also busy during the day with other friends dropping by. People like to talk to Phyllis and to be around her. They know she cares about them and their needs. How do they know? She listens. Her face gives her full attention to those she is with as does her mind and heart. She asks questions and is willing to hear the answers, even negative ones. Nothing shocks her. Nothing you say will make her end your friendship. You feel safe with her because she listens.

Listening is not merely a matter of personality for Phyllis or the rest of us. It is a decision to act in a loving way. Today she told me the doorbell rang just when she had plans to get a jump on the housework. Her heart sank to see friends at the door. Despite her desire to shoo them away, she once more chose to give her ear and time to them.

Third, Jesus showed his love *by sharing the truth with his disciples.* God could have chosen to let us stumble haphazardly on bits of truth here and there, not even knowing when we had found something that was certain. Instead he revealed his truth to us so that we would know how to live in harmony with the universe and with its Creator. Jesus opened God's Word in a way that had never been done before. This was an act of love that Jesus took at great risk. Though it may seem that everyone wants the truth, such is not the case. We do not want to read newspaper stories about starving millions. We do not want our politicians to tell us that we will all need to sacrifice to solve our country's problems. We do not want to hear that our society is racist. We put people who tell us such things out of business, out of office or out of this world.

Those who do love, who do desire what is best for others, will tell the truth. Which is the loving response? To tell an overweight friend with high blood pressure that he is killing himself? Or to help him laugh off his problem with another piece of cake? Which is more loving? To tell an unrepentant friend with no interest in God that she is cutting herself off from eternal life? Or to help her laugh it off with a Hollywood comedy about heaven? Genuine love can cost hurt feelings or even a friendship. Do we love that much? Jesus did and it cost him his reputation, his following and eventually his life.

Fourth, Jesus loved his disciples *by being open with them about himself.* In the upper room, the night before he died, Jesus told them, "No longer do I call you servants, for the servant does not know what his master is doing; but I have called you friends, for all that I have heard from my Father I have made known to you" (Jn 15:15). We are not sanctified computers, performing duties only at the behest of our Celestial Programmer. We are people God has chosen as his partners in a great enterprise. "He has made known to us in all wisdom and insight the mystery of his will" (Eph 1:9). He has revealed his plan to us which was hidden for ages. We, frail, finite, fickle humans are colaborers with the Almighty, Infinite, Sovereign Lord of the Universe. Unbelievable! Yet it is so.

Jesus also shared the intimate details of his death and resurrection with the disciples, those things which were most central to his earthly mission. This made it more than his plan or the Father's plan. This made it theirs too—and ours as the church.

We feel wanted and appreciated when we are included. We always want to be chosen early when teams are being divided. When we have been consulted on a family, business or church matter, we are more likely to support the final decision (even if we disagree with it) than if an edict comes down from the top that we are to carry out. The reason? Those in authority have shown their love for us by soliciting our opinion.

I continually fight the urge not to share information with

others, to keep decisions in a closed circle. When I fail to share information, people feel hurt and left out, even though I may have increased my own illusion of self-importance and power. When I do share information, people feel included and their performance improves.

Jesus also openly sought the support and help of his disciples in his heaviest hour. He asked them to stay awake and to pray with him in the Garden of Gethsemane. He revealed his need, his vulnerability. He did not pretend he had no pain or anguish over what he was about to face. And in so doing he showed us how to face trials and hard choices. If he had been closed, the lesson would have been lost. We too can be of more help to others by being open about our problems than by creating a false front of perfection.

Last, Jesus showed the disciples his love *by dying for them.* "Greater love has no man than this, that a man lay down his life for his friends" (Jn 15:13). "I am the good shepherd. The good shepherd lays down his life for the sheep" (Jn 10:11). He died that we might live.

We too show our love for others when we sacrifice ourselves. We may not be called on to give our lives. But we will certainly be asked to give our time, our ambitions, our conveniences, our money, laying them down for the flock. This is, of course, nothing more than what all Christians are called to, in humility counting others better than ourselves (Phil 2:3).

Jesus left a model for us to follow, a model of love shown by his prayer, his listening, his teaching, his openness and his death. We are to follow his lead so that we too can say to those we leave, "Love one another as I have loved you" (Jn 16:12).

7
The Path
of
Envisioning

*Be Thou my Vision, O Lord of my heart; naught be all else
to me save that thou art.*
Ancient Irish Hymn

Thomas Sine tells of the time he visited a pastor who was talking expansively about his church's building plans.

"Tom, we're building the best educational facility money can buy."

"Roy, how much are houses running now?" Tom asked.

"It's ridiculous! They start at $150,000."

"So who is buying?"

"Mainly older couples."

"And do they have children?"

"If they do, they're usually college age."

"Roy, who will be using this new facility when it's built?"

The pastor apparently lost most of the color in his face and nearly all of it from his hair as well. It had not occurred to him that he was building an educational facility in what soon would be a childless area.[1]

An obvious error? Yes, but we all fail to think ahead at times, fail to calculate the effects of our decisions and actions. Large doses of DDT may be quite effective in stamping out certain pests. But what happens when the poison starts seeping into our water table? We lack vision.

Vision, of course, is the ability to see. We speak of being short-sighted when we don't anticipate what will or could happen based on what already is happening. Sometimes we are so used to seeing things a certain way, we can't see what is really there. The eight most deadly words in any group are, "But that's the way we've always done it."

When my father died and it was time to make plans, I told the pastor we wanted a small graveside service in the morning followed by a church service. As simple as it was, I had to repeat our request several times before he finally seemed to understand. He had never come across that pattern before. Previously the graveside service had always followed the funeral. But afterward he said, "I don't know why more people don't do it that way. When the grave is the end of all the plans, it can leave you so barren and desolate. But if the funeral is last, you leave with the whole Christian community with you, supporting you."

Yet so often our minds are closed in by mounds of rock and vegetation. We have not opened ourselves to see the world in new ways. It is often more comfortable and secure to maintain an old pattern. We know what to expect as do others. So we resist change. But the world continues to change despite our best efforts, and so we continually need to see life anew.

Beyond Myopia

One man who did not suffer from such myopia was Robert Raikes, the editor of *The Gloucester Journal* in eighteenth-century England. Statues in his honor are found in London and Toronto. Schools have been named after him and books written about him. One of his friends even considered him the most important man since the Reformers of the sixteenth century.[2] His influence is still felt today by millions around the world. To what does he owe all this renown?

Eighteenth-century England was a genteel, civilized society— but only for the privileged few. Despite England's advances over many other countries at the time, the vast majority of its population was poor. A harsh class system prevailed. Cities were beginning to grow as industrialization took hold. But conditions grew worse.

Raikes was a man of firm evangelical commitment who "used his newspaper to influence public opinion in favor of the suffering lower class, and he was largely responsible for the improvement of prison conditions in England at the close of the century."[3] In the process of committing himself to prison reform, he discovered another related problem.

Because the poorer classes were rarely considered fit for education, many urban children worked twelve- and fifteen-hour days, six days a week, in factories. On the seventh day, bands of children would then roam the city and outlying areas unsupervised, vandalizing, fighting and stealing. Raikes wrote, "I was struck with concern after seeing a group of children wretchedly ragged, at play in the streets."[4] So in 1780 he and Thomas Stork, rector of St. John the Baptist Church in Gloucester, worked to teach ninety children for several hours each Sunday. Raikes promoted the idea constantly in the *Journal,* and by 1786 two-hundred thousand children throughout England were enrolled in Sunday schools of various kinds.[5] By 1831, the movement grew to a reported 1,250,000 children.[6]

Raikes saw this massive problem as an opportunity for bettering the lot of the lower classes by teaching them to read and write, by giving them direct contact with the Bible (in contrast to the usual catechetical teaching of the day), and by seeking to change the children from ruffians to committed Christians. He combined social conscience with an evangelistic emphasis that is an apt model for our day as well. The prejudices against teaching the lower classes were strong. And while Raikes and his comrades bore much of the culture's attitude toward the poor, they did not allow these prejudices to prevent them from pursuing their path.[7] What others saw as a broken fence or a ragged group of children, Raikes saw as a way to transform the country.

A Troika of Tyrants

Our vision is often so crowded with the trivialities and urgencies of the day that we never see many opportunities. *The bus broke down. The accompanist can't make it to rehearsal. Money is short. My mother is having surgery. A paper is due.* We are so caught up in patching leaks that we don't see that the ship is headed for an iceberg. Our fast-paced world is not conducive to contemplation and reflection. Crisis management (of family life and of international relations) is actually our standard operating procedure.

Another constant struggle for me is choosing among all the good things I can do. I enjoy volleyball. I enjoy choir. I enjoy work. I enjoy family. I enjoy reading. I enjoy writing. I enjoy resting. But I can't do them all—at least not as much as I'd like.

Overchoice hits organizations and groups as well. There are more social events a church could have than there are days in a year. There are billions of dollars' worth of needs in the world to contribute to. There are hundreds of hurting people in the community.

How can we maintain a vision for our church, our school, our group, our family or our committee in the midst of these overwhelming needs and possibilities?

But this is not the end of problems for envisioning. Expectations (especially negative ones) can be a nuisance. If I expect the junior-high class to bear a remarkable resemblance to Raikes's ruffians, they will have an uncanny way of doing so. If I expect the group president to do all the budgetary work, I will be very upset when I find out she expected me to. If I expect, on the other hand, to have many opportunities for witnessing, I probably will.

And what if everyone in my group seems to have a different expectation of what our group should be? How can you implant and nurture a vision in others that will incorporate diversity, maintain unity and still help the group grow? If one person in a boat rows one way and another rows another, you have diversity (two directions) and unity (both are rowing), but you never get anywhere.

Some people have a natural ability to overcome the tyrannical troika of crisis, overchoice and expectations. Amid the flurry of conflicting needs and pressures, they can instantly see the overarching principle or program which unifies and answers diverse problems and sets a grand new course. For a second group of people with more limited natural resources, in which I include myself, to achieve the same result requires hours of analysis, agonizing over alternatives and painfully planning. But in either case visions that can look beyond immediate problems and focus on what is truly important generally possess a few basic characteristics.

First, these visions are big. They are larger than life, larger than ourselves. They take us outside our own immediate concerns and move us into the rest of life.

In *Dedication and Leadership,* Douglas Hyde, who was converted to Christianity after years as a Communist worker in Britain, analyzes why the Communists have been so successful and asks what the church can learn from this. Hyde writes, "Marx concluded his Communist Manifesto with the words 'You have a world to win.' Here is a tremendous aim. In material terms, one could hardly aim higher. The belief that the world is there to be won and that Communists can win it is firmly implanted in the mind of every Communist cadre. It is with him all the time. . . . The Christian may say that the Communists have the worst creed on earth. But what they have to appreciate is that the Communists shout it from the house-tops; whilst too often those who believe they have the best speak with a muted voice when they speak at all."[8]

The Communists have a goal which captures the imagination. It grips the mind and motivates the body to act. It also allows for a wide variety of ways of achieving the goal: argument, force, propaganda, even democratic processes. But whatever the method, the goal remains.

Contrast this to the all-too-frequent goals of a young couple: monetary security, a big house in the suburbs, handsome children. Yet when these are achieved, nothing is left. Twenty years of marriage end in divorce. Their vision was not big enough. It was only as large as themselves.

Second, a worthy vision must be personal. A large vision can be fine. But if it is too abstract or too distant, no one will follow. A vision must touch our lives at some point, compelling our involvement.

Again let me quote from Hyde. "The [Communist] recruit is made to feel that there is a great battle going on all over the world. That this includes his own country, his own town, his own neighbourhood, the block of flats in which he lives, the factory or office where he works. He is made to feel also that the period of history in which he happens to be living is a decisive one and that he personally has a decisive role to play."[9]

Winning the world is bigger than I am, but it includes me too. I am part of it. I belong. It relates to the news I hear, the food I eat, the people I talk to, the goods I buy, the way I live life.

Many people have come to Christ on the misapprehension that they can be saved and not change anything about the way they live. On the contrary, everything is different. I no longer own my clothes. They are Christ's, and he may require that I give some away. My time is not my own. It is Christ's, and he will rule over how each hour is spent. I am no longer a slave to sin but a slave to God. As a Christian, I am caught in a vision that is as personal as my thoughts. The vision is large, yes. But it is not unattainable. By God acting in me, I bring it closer to reality.

Third, a worthy vision is simple. It is not a complex theorem. It does not require a Ph.D. (or two or three) to understand it. It is concise and complete. "Every Communist cadre . . . has a clear goal. He knows what he is working for."[10]

Theology and biblical studies are wonderful disciplines. Their depth shows in a limited way the infinite depth and breadth and height of the God we serve. Yet in the depth of our study we must never forget the rock on which we stand.

Once the German theologian Karl Barth, who had written thousands of pages of theological works and thought and studied Christianity for decades, was asked to summarize the essence of his work. Without hesitation he answered, "Jesus loves me; this I know, for the Bible tells me so." In the midst of his complexity and profundity, he had not lost the simplicity of the message we have been given.

Many find it helpful to put their personal or group goal in a theme. A theme for a conference. A verse for a family. A catch phrase for a class. A motto for the year. Simple enough to remember, it gives a common bond to all who put themselves under it.

Fourth, a worthy vision must be true. Hitler inspired millions with a large, personal and simple lie. Christianity requires that a vision be true. By this I mean more than propositional truth, though it must include that as well. We in the West with our Greek ways of thinking are seldom weak here. Rather we often fall when it comes to living truth. Our vision must be rooted in the person of God, his character, his being. It must be consistent with who he is, the great "I AM." So must our vision be.

The life of Christ itself showed his vision to be rooted in his Father. As I have mentioned previously, Jesus' priorities were clear during his ministry on earth: his devotion to his Father and his concern for people. In Mark 1:35-38 he withdrew to pray and in the process was renewed to go to other cities that needed his message. Again after a tiring day, he went alone to pray (Mk 6:46). As we saw in John 13:3 he had a clear concept of where he had come from (the Father), of where he was going (back to the Father) and of all that had been given into his hands (his mission to the world).

This does not mean Christ's energies and attention were divided. They were one. Often we consider our devotional life, our quiet time, as an end in itself—praying to God, listening to him in meditation, steeping ourselves in the Scriptures. This is by no means the whole of spirituality. Our involvement with the Word drives us and empowers us for action in the world. Our involvement in the world likewise throws us back to God in dependence on his grace when we are weak and on his truth when we are confused. One is only complete with the other.

Paul's Vision

I have enjoyed going back and back to Paul's letter to the Ephesians because it more succinctly and powerfully communicates the Christian vision than any other of his letters. While most of Paul's letters are directed to the particular problems of a given church (the Judaizers in Galatia or the Jewish/Gentile problems in Rome, for example), this one seems blissfully free from turmoil. In it Paul gives his most complete picture of the Christian world view.

Some scholars believe the letter has this character because it was not written solely for the church at Ephesus but to several congregations in the area with a variety of circumstances. They point out that no individuals are mentioned or greeted by name. (Quite a contrast to his other letters.) So instead of addressing a specific situation, he writes in broad strokes about the Christian faith.

The letter most likely was addressed very generally "to the saints who are also faithful in Christ Jesus" (1:1). Many ancient manuscripts do read, "to the saints who are at Ephesus and faithful in Christ Jesus." This is perhaps because several copies of the letter were made (one for each church) with room left to fill in the name of the particular church. While apparently some manuscripts were never addressed to a particular church, the one addressed to the Ephesians survived. Additional copies of the Ephesian letter were made and circulated, and thus the letter received its name. In any case, Paul took this opportunity to impart his vision.

He takes very little time to get to the heart of God's plan for the ages. "He has made known to us in all wisdom and insight the mystery of his will, according to his purpose which he set forth in Christ as a plan for the fulness of time, to unite all things in him, things in heaven and things on earth" (1:9-10). As I mentioned earlier, God has revealed to us that he intends to bring the entire universe together in Christ. He will be the one Lord of all that exists. No divisions, no rebellions, no party factions, no arguments, no splits, no schisms. All will be one in Christ.

What a glorious vision! What a magnificent picture! The Communists have a world to win; God has a cosmos. The entire creation, seen and unseen, will be brought into harmony and unity in Christ. Still more startling is the next sentence. "In him, according to the purpose of him who accomplishes all things according to the counsel of his will, we who first hoped in Christ have been destined and appointed to live for the praise of his glory" (1:11-12). Is that

possible? Are we really to be part of this plan to bring everything
together in Christ? Why would God choose us? We are finite and
fallen. It all seems too hard to believe.

So Paul goes on to pray just this, that his readers will believe it
and see the vision he sees. "I do not cease to give thanks for you,
remembering you in my prayers, that the God of our Lord Jesus
Christ, the Father of glory, may give you a spirit of wisdom and of
revelation in the knowledge of him, having the eyes of your hearts
enlightened, that you may know what is the hope to which he has
called you, what are the riches of his glorious inheritance in the
saints, and what is the immeasurable greatness of his power in us
who believe" (1:16-19). He wants "the eyes of your hearts enlightened." He wants our vision expanded to believe that our calling is
indeed to be part of God's great plan for the universe. But how can
we help? Weak as we are, we have immense power in us. How much
power? As much power as was "in Christ when he raised him from
the dead and made him sit at his right hand" (1:20). The force that
resurrected Jesus is in us. We face no energy crisis as Christians.
Our supply is as limitless as God himself. And just as our salvation is
a gift from God (2:8), so is the power to do good works (2:10).

How do we know all this will happen? How do we know all will
be one in Christ? Because, says Paul, it is already happening. The
foretaste, the first instance of the unity of all things, is found in the
church. God has reconciled Gentiles who were once "separated
from Christ, alienated from the commonwealth of Israel, and
strangers to the covenants of promise, having no hope and without
God in the world" (2:12). They "who once were far off have been
brought near in the blood of Christ" (2:13). Yet God not only reconciled Gentiles to himself, he also overcame centuries of antagonism
and made Gentiles one with Jews who had come to consider them
virtually subhuman, antihuman infidels. "Christ . . . is our peace,
who has made us both one, and has broken down the dividing wall

of hostility . . . that he might create in himself one new man in place of the two" (2:13-15). He has not made the Gentiles into Jews. No. One new man is created, replacing and encompassing both of the old. And if God can overcome the wall that separated Jews and Gentiles, will he not also be able to do so with the rest of the universe? This immense vision was not clear until the coming of Christ. "The mystery of Christ . . . was not made known to the sons of men in other generations as it has now been revealed . . . ; that is, how the Gentiles are fellow heirs, members of the same body, and partakers of the promise in Christ Jesus through the gospel" (3:4-6). Now it is clear that God's goal is to achieve utter oneness through the work of his Son, Jesus.

Indeed this very unity of Jews and Gentiles in one church "is the plan of the mystery hidden for ages in God who created all things; that through the church the manifold wisdom of God might now be made known" (3:9-10). Through the church and the unity God has created in it, both the world and "the principalities and powers in the heavenly places" will learn God's plan for eternity (3:10). Not only is the church the foretaste of cosmic unity. It is the divinely appointed means for achieving this.

At this Paul is thrust into a prayer of praise that calls for God to be glorified "in the church and in Christ Jesus to all generations, for ever and ever. Amen" (3:21). The vision is as large as the universe, far beyond our finite concerns. The vision is personal. Indeed it envelopes us. We are brothers and sisters of people all over the globe. Race, geography, social status, language do not divide us from our fellow Christians. Whether we want to or not, we will be wrapped up in the unity God has ordained for all creation. Yet we also participate now in the union God has worked in the church, being reconciled to him and to others who would otherwise be our enemies. The vision is simple. All will be one in Christ. The vision is true. It is rooted in the very nature of God, his oneness, and in his compassion for people.

Our visions must be the same. They need not be cosmic or even worldwide to be larger than ourselves. If we anchor ourselves in who Christ is and in the needs of others, we can hardly miss. Starting a food co-op in a low-income housing project, inviting an elderly widow to be your adopted grandmother for a family night, taking time to study and pray regularly with a new Christian—all are steps consistent with the bigness, the personalness, the simplicity and the truth of our God.

Whatever the step, a step must be taken to make a vision more than a passing wish. J. Oswald Sanders says, "The man who possesses vision must do something about it or he will remain visionary, not a leader."[11] Paul starts to apply his vision at just this level when he moves into the practical half of his letter. "Maintain the unity of the Spirit in the bond of peace" (4:3). How? "With all lowliness and meekness, with patience, forbearing one another in love" (4:2). Why? "There is one body and one Spirit, just as you were called to the one hope that belongs to your call, one Lord, one faith, one baptism, one God and Father of us all, who is above all and through all and in all" (4:4-6).

This sevenfold oneness does not obliterate our individuality. "Grace was given to each" (4:7). He gave us gifts fit for each person ("some should be apostles, some prophets, some evangelists, some pastors and teachers"—4:11) but all with the same goal ("to equip the saints for the work of ministry, for building up the body of Christ, until we all attain to the unity of the faith"—4:12-13).

Paul knows, however, that giving others the tools to help the church grow is not a mere business transaction. So much money buys so much goods. As James knew, our fallen human nature can turn the glow of even the simplest Christian gathering into a firestorm (Jas 3:5-6). Paul cautions, "Speaking the truth in love, . . .

putting away falsehood, let every one speak the truth with his neighbor" (4:15-25). What can break the bond of peace quicker than a sarcastic word? Even a true word (perhaps about some wrong forgiven but not quite forgotten) that is not spoken in love can drive Christians apart.

Paul continues, "Let no evil talk come out of your mouths, but only such as is good for edifying. . . . Let all bitterness and wrath and anger and clamor and slander be put away from you, with all malice, and be kind to one another, tenderhearted, forgiving one another, as God in Christ forgave you" (4:29, 31-32). When there is evil talk and bitterness, there is no unity. But when kindness and forgiveness reign, God's peace dwells with us also.

Paul goes on to discuss the union of husband and wife (5:21-33), of children and parents (6:1-4), and of slaves and masters (6:5-9) before giving his closing exhortation and benediction.

I have taken some time to trace Paul's vision in Ephesians for several reasons. I find it a stirring look at the universe from God's perspective. It is also a vivid example of what our visions can be like. It is practical as well, touching our every word and our dearest relationships (church, spouse, family, work). It is also double-rooted in the needs of others and in the being of God. As we guide others toward growth in Christ, the focus of our vision must be our Lord and nothing else.

8
The
Path
Together

Because God has bound us together in one body with other Christians in Jesus Christ, long before we entered into common life with them, we enter into that common life not as demanders but as thankful recipients.
Dietrich Bonhoeffer

By now, having read the previous seven chapters, you are either exhilarated and ready to lead the world or you are depressed and ready to give up.

If you are exhilarated, you are challenged by the paths of leadership I have suggested. You see nothing but possibilities for service, following, facilitating, teaching, modeling and envisioning. You can't wait to help others in any way possible, meeting whatever needs they have—and maybe even some they don't. If this is you, I have a word of caution.

On the other hand, you may be overwhelmed by the size of the role ahead for you. You know your selfishness and how reluctant to serve you are. You know your limited teaching skills and inability to envision. Sure, maybe you are good at encouraging others and can facilitate pretty well, but being a model of the Christian life? No way. If this is you, I have a word of hope.

The word of hope and the word of caution is, interestingly, the same for both groups. And even if you find yourself somewhere in between, this word is for you too.

No one is a perfect leader.

Even less than that. No one fulfills the six leadership roles I've discussed in this book in a full and balanced manner. God has certainly given many men and women many abilities and strengths, but none is a self-contained leader, and we should not expect ourselves to be either.

Those of you who like tracing themes will no doubt have already picked up a hint of one in the last paragraph that I have hit upon many times throughout this book. Leadership is not a one-man or a one-woman show. It is a group effort. By definition, leading is a kind of interaction within a group. A group of one needs (and can have) no leader.

If, therefore, it is impossible for one person to fulfill all the leadership roles of a group, what is the solution? Group leadership. Someone who is a gifted teacher may not be an adequate facilitator. Someone who can communicate a dynamic vision may not be able to model effectively. But people need all these kinds of leadership to meet their wide variety of needs and move toward their goals. Group leadership can accomplish all this. In the chapter on teaching I discussed how several people have had a profound impact on me, each in different ways. Their combined effect, I hope, has made me a more balanced, more whole person than if just one had influenced me. Likewise a group and the individuals in it need a similar broad-based leadership.

Just as the body of Christ functions by the unique gifts of all its members working together, so the human leadership of the body of Christ should be a body. The leadership team of a group pool their various gifts to guide the larger body. One contributes encouragement, another the ability to perceive needs, another the willingness to do whatever is called for.

"Impossible," you say. "Unworkable." On the contrary, families often offer perfect illustrations. God has so ordered it that opposites attract. So one may be pragmatic and the other a dreamer. One may be sensitive and the other thoughtful. One may be good with numbers (and checkbooks) and the other with creating a comfortable and beautiful home. One senses God's direction, and the other finds ways to fulfill it.

Even children add to the mix. Young ones help us enjoy the small pleasures God has given us—rocks and leaves. Older ones help keep our priorities clear by asking penetrating (and occasionally uncomfortable) questions about why we do things as we do.

A group need not necessarily have two, three or more leaders at the same time to achieve the same result (though this would seem most normal). It could rotate leadership in the group based on the need of the group at a particular time and the gifts of the members. The leader of a group that is just starting might be the one who can help solidify a vision. Once this is complete, the teacher might assume leadership if that was called for. The facilitator might then help the group put into action what they had been taught.

How leadership works out in practice is not nearly as important as *that* it work out. Leaders who believe they must be on top, alone, only hurt those they lead by not allowing them to grow in the fullness of God's plan. We are finite as individuals. But as a group, we become the body of Christ himself, in all his strength and power and grace and love.

Another way of saying that leadership is a group effort is this:

everyone leads. It may sound like anarchy. But that's not what I mean by the phrase. Certainly not everyone is a designated leader. One person ultimately should fulfill that important and legitimate role. One person needs to be accountable for the character and actions of the group. But such designated leaders need to realize that the total burden does not rest on them. It is shared, and one of their primary duties is to see that all actually do participate in the leadership of the group. That, to a great extent, is what I meant by *facilitating* in chapter four.

Thus, by "everyone leads" I mean that everyone, at one time or another, fulfills a leadership role (not necessarily a leadership position). Some help meet needs or group goals more than others. But everyone does some. A word of encouragement. A suggestion. An act of thoughtfulness. An insight. A commitment. A dream. All these shared with others by ordinary Christians seeking to follow their Lord are all acts of leadership—or can be.

This is not automatic Nirvana, however. David Mains cautions against overemphasizing the equality and value of every member of the body. He writes, "In setting up [Circle Church], I had deliberately played down authority structures and invested power in a broadly based board, not in the pastor. Our members came with an anti-authoritarian bias, and I consented to it. And when it finally came to the place where I said, 'I'm sorry, but for the sake of the body I must take this action,' they couldn't follow me."[1] So little teaching had been done on spiritual authority, the people forgot how to follow.

The Bible's teaching on authority is important, as I tried to emphasize in chapter three. We cannot forget that we are under authority as we work and pray together. We must respect those God has placed over us and whom we have placed ourselves under. As a group we must all learn to follow as well as to lead.

But just as common as Christians who don't know how to follow are those in designated positions of leadership who inhibit and squash initiative in others as they seek to express what God has given them. Strong leadership of this kind does not produce a strong group. It produces weak members who are not allowed to grow.

Just as birds must be pushed out of their nests to strengthen their wings, learn to fly and fulfill the birdhood God has given them, so must we all be given opportunities to stretch into new experiences and grow into full maturity. And that opportunity to grow is far more important than a well-executed flight.

This is so easy for me to forget. I *know* I can give a better talk, prepare a better discussion, give better comfort, plan a better program or pray a better prayer than someone with far less experience than me. But the growth of others is more important than a well-executed flight—or talk or discussion or program or prayer. People come before projects.

Besides that, I may be wrong in the first place. I may not do the better job. God may work through another in a way he could not work through me. My very arrogance may be a barrier to effective ministry.

Leadership is a path of many paths. It is a road traveled by many people together—as a body. The destination of maturity in Christ, however, is not reached by merely arriving at the end of the road. Our goal is achieved by making the journey itself. The path of leadership is one such trek.

Notes

Chapter 1 Paths of Leadership
[1]James MacGregor Burns, *Leadership* (New York: Harper & Row, 1978), p. 251.

Chapter 2 The Path of Serving
[1]Robert J. Ringer, *Looking Out for Number One* (New York: Funk & Wagnalls, 1977), pp. 33, 37-38.
[2]Franklin D. Roosevelt, quoted in Burns, *Leadership*, p. xi.
[3]J. I. Packer, *Knowing God* (Downers Grove, Ill.: InterVarsity Press, 1973), p. 187.
[4]Udo Middelmann, *Pro-Existence* (Downers Grove, Ill.: InterVarsity Press, 1974), p. 30.
[5]John R. W. Stott, *Who Is My Neighbor?* (Downers Grove, Ill.: InterVarsity Press, 1975), pp. 18-19.

Chapter 3 The Path of Following
[1]Other related passages in John not mentioned in the text are 5:43; 7:28; 8:54; 10:25; 12:49; 13:3; 14:10-31; 15:10; 16:13; 17:2.
[2]Howard Butt, *The Velvet Covered Brick* (San Francisco: Harper & Row, 1973), p. 59.

[3]Henri Nouwen, *The Wounded Healer* (New York: Doubleday, 1972), pp. 72-73.

[4]Butt, *The Velvet Covered Brick,* pp. 61-62, from Paul Torgeson, *A Concept of Organization* (New York: American Book-Van Nostrand, 1969), p. 54.

Chapter 4 The Path of Facilitating

[1]Richard Adams, *Watership Down* (New York: Macmillan, 1972), p. 23.

[2]Ibid., p. 110.

[3]Ibid., p. 168.

[4]I owe the idea of studying the group dynamics in *Watership Down* to Paul Tokunaga.

[5]Ibid., p. 404.

[6]John Powell, *The Secret of Staying in Love* (Niles, Ill.: Argus, 1974), pp. 15-16.

[7]John White, *Daring to Draw Near* (Downers Grove, Ill.: InterVarsity Press, 1977), pp. 132-33.

Chapter 7 The Path of Envisioning

[1]Thomas W. Sine, Jr., "Heeding the Signals of the Future," *Voices* (Fall 1981), p. 3.

[2]Robert W. Lynn and Elliot Wright, *The Big Little School: 200 Years of the Sunday School* (Birmingham: Religious Education Press; Nashville: Abingdon, 1980), p. 24.

[3]Elmer L. Towns, "Robert Raikes (1735-1811)," in *A History of Religious Educators,* ed. Elmer L. Towns (Grand Rapids, Mich.: Baker, 1975), p. 229.

[4]Quoted in Towns, "Robert Raikes," from *Gentleman's Magazine* (1784).

[5]G. G. Thorne, Jr., "Raikes, Robert (1735-1811)," in *The New International Dictionary of the Christian Church,* ed. J. D. Douglas (Grand Rapids, Mich.: Zondervan, 1974), p. 82.

[6]Towns, "Robert Raikes," p. 235.

[7]Ibid., p. 230.

[8]Douglas Hyde, *Dedication and Leadership* (Notre Dame: University of Notre Dame Press, 1966), pp. 31-32.

[9]Ibid., p. 52.

[10]Ibid., p. 31.

[11]J. Oswald Sanders, *Spiritual Leadership* (Chicago: Moody Press, 1962), p. 53.

Chapter 8 The Path Together

[1]David Mains with Philip Yancey, "My Greatest Ministry Mistakes," *Leadership* 1, no. 2 (Spring 1980), p. 20.